MAPWORK SKILLS AND LOCAL ISSUES

by
Jack Gillett

The GCSE/Key Stage 4 successor to *Map Reading and Local Studies in Colour*
by A P Fullagar and H E Virgo

Hodder & Stoughton

LONDON SYDNEY AUCKLAND TORONTO

Acknowledgements

The publisher would like to thank the following for their permission to reproduce photographs in this book:

Aerofilms Ltd (1.8B, 2.4F, 3.6A, 3.8H); CEGB (National Power) (3.6C and D); D. Coutts (1.3A, 1.8A); Durham County Council (3.2C and D); K. Grimwade (2.3F); J. Heyes (2.6A(2) and (3)); ICCE Photography (1.5A); C. R. Jakes (3.1D); Jefferson Air Photography (3.7A); L. Kimpton (1.6A(2), 1.7H, 2.3F, 3.2E); King's Lynn and West Norfolk Borough Council (3.1E); C. Martin (2.4B, 2.4D); A. Moore (1.6A(5)); Ordnance Survey (1.5B); Jason Smalley (3.7B); D. Taylor (3.3C); United Kingdom Atomic Energy Authority (2.4E); Dr A. M. Warnes (1.6A(7)).

Every effort has been made to trace and acknowledge correctly all copyright holders, but if any have been overlooked the publishers will be pleased to make the necessary arrangements at the first opportunity.

British Library Cataloguing in Publication Data
Gillett, Jack
  Mapwork skills and local issues.
  1. Map reading
  I. Title
  912'.01'4
ISBN 0 340 50560 5

First published 1990

© 1990 Jack Gillett

First published in Great Britain as *Map Reading and Local Studies in Colour* 1967. Second edition 1975. Third edition 1984.

Typeset by Taurus Graphics, Abingdon, Oxon.
Printed in Great Britain for Hodder and Stoughton Educational, a division of Hodder and Stoughton Ltd, Mill Road, Dunton Green, Sevenoaks, Kent by Colorcraft Ltd, Hong Kong.

For Kath and Terry

Contents

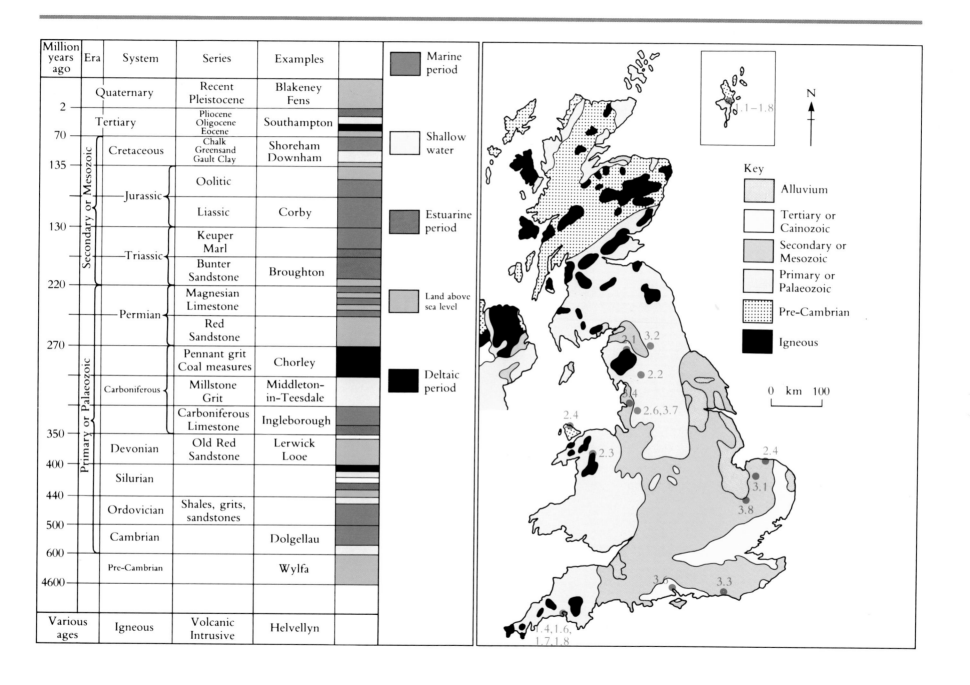

Million years ago	Era	System	Series	Examples		
		Quaternary	Recent	Blakeney		Marine period
2			Pleistocene	Fens		
70		Tertiary	Pliocene Oligocene Eocene	Southampton		Shallow water
135	Secondary or Mesozoic	Cretaceous	Chalk Greensand Gault Clay	Shoreham Downham		
		Jurassic	Oolitic			Estuarine period
130			Liassic	Corby		
		Triassic	Keuper Marl			
220			Bunter Sandstone	Broughton		Land above sea level
270	Primary or Palaeozoic	Permian	Magnesian Limestone			
			Red Sandstone			
		Carboniferous	Pennant grit Coal measures	Chorley		Deltaic period
			Millstone Grit	Middleton-in-Teesdale		
350			Carboniferous Limestone	Ingleborough		
400		Devonian	Old Red Sandstone	Lerwick Looe		
440		Silurian				
500		Ordovician	Shales, grits, sandstones			
600		Cambrian		Dolgellau		
4600		Pre-Cambrian		Wylfa		
Various ages		Igneous	Volcanic Intrusive	Helvellyn		

Key

- Alluvium
- Tertiary or Cainozoic
- Secondary or Mesozoic
- Primary or Palaeozoic
- Pre-Cambrian
- Igneous

Geological map of Britain. The unit numbers show the areas studied in this book

3

Ordnance Survey Symbol Charts

Key for 1:50 000 maps

ROADS AND PATHS
Not necessarily rights of way

Service area M 1 — Elevated — Motorway (dual carriageway)

Junction number 1

Motorway under construction

Unfenced — Footbridge — Trunk road
A 40 (T)

Dual carriageway — Main road
A 487

Main road under construction

Secondary road
B 4313

Narrow road with passing places
A 855 — B 885

Bridge — Road generally more than 4 m wide

Road generally less than 4 m wide

Other road, drive or track

Path

Gradient: 1 in 5 and steeper   1 in 7 to 1 in 5

Gates   Road tunnel

Ferry P — Ferry V — Ferry (passenger)   Ferry (vehicle)

PUBLIC RIGHTS OF WAY
(Not applicable to Scotland)

·················· Footpath

– – – – – – Bridleway

–·–·–·–·– Road used as a public path

-+-+-+-+-+- Byway open to all traffic

Public rights of way indicated by these symbols have been
derived from Definitive Maps as amended by later enactments
or instruments held by Ordnance Survey on 1st June 1983
and are shown subject to the limitations imposed by the scale
of mapping

**The representation on this map of any other road, track or
path is no evidence of the existence of a right of way**

Danger Area   MOD Ranges in the area.   Danger!   Observe warning notices

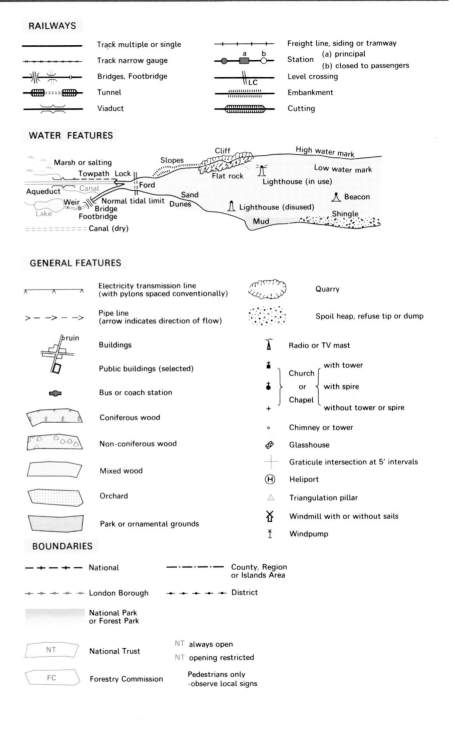

RAILWAYS

——— Track multiple or single

——— Track narrow gauge

—||— Bridges, Footbridge

—▒▒— Tunnel

——— Viaduct

—┼—┼— Freight line, siding or tramway

●—■—○ Station   (a) principal   (b) closed to passengers

—LC— Level crossing

——— Embankment

——— Cutting

WATER FEATURES

Marsh or salting   Slopes   Cliff   High water mark
Towpath Lock   Low water mark
Aqueduct Canal Ford   Lighthouse (in use)
Weir   Normal tidal limit   Sand   Beacon
Lake   Bridge   Dunes   Lighthouse (disused)   Shingle
          Footbridge   Mud

– – – – – Canal (dry)

GENERAL FEATURES

×—×—× Electricity transmission line (with pylons spaced conventionally)

>–->–-> Pipe line (arrow indicates direction of flow)

bruin Buildings

Public buildings (selected)

Bus or coach station

Coniferous wood

Non-coniferous wood

Mixed wood

Orchard

Park or ornamental grounds

Quarry

Spoil heap, refuse tip or dump

Radio or TV mast

Church or Chapel { with tower / with spire / without tower or spire }

○ Chimney or tower

Glasshouse

Graticule intersection at 5' intervals

(H) Heliport

△ Triangulation pillar

Windmill with or without sails

Windpump

BOUNDARIES

—+—+— National

—●—●—● London Borough

National Park or Forest Park

NT National Trust

FC Forestry Commission

—·—·— County, Region or Islands Area

—+—+—+ District

NT always open
NT opening restricted

Pedestrians only -observe local signs

ABBREVIATIONS

P	Post office	CH	Clubhouse
PH	Public house	PC	Public convenience (in rural areas)
MS	Milestone	TH	Town Hall, Guildhall or equivalent
MP	Milepost	CG	Coastguard

ANTIQUITIES

 VILLA Roman   ⚔ Battlefield (with date)   + Position of antiquity which cannot be drawn to scale

 Castle Non-Roman   ☆ Tumulus

🜲 Ancient Monuments and Historic Buildings in the care of the Secretaries of State for the Environment, for Scotland and for Wales and that are open to the public

The revision date of archaeological information varies over the sheet

HEIGHTS

—50— Contours are at 10 metres vertical interval

•144 Heights are to the nearest metre above mean sea level

Heights shown close to a triangulation pillar refer to the station height at ground level and not necessarily to the summit.

ROCK FEATURES

outcrop

cliff

scree

VEGETATION

 Park, Fenced   Orchard

Wood, Coniferous, Fenced   Furze

Wood, Non-Coniferous, Unfenced   Rough Pasture Heath & Moor

Brushwood, Fenced & Unfenced   Osier Bed

Reeds

TOURIST AND LEISURE INFORMATION

⛺ Camp Site		PC Public Convenience (in rural areas)
🚐 Caravan Site		Station (special interest)
🅿 Parking		⊕ Mountain Rescue Post
⚑ Golf Course or Links		▲ Youth Hostel
✕ Picnic Site		🛈 Information Centre
Viewpoint		*Manor* Selected places of interest
		SAILING
☎ T Public Telephone		☎ A R Motoring Organisation Telephone

On page 51 the contours are at 25 feet vertical interval.

Key for 1:25 000 maps

ROADS AND PATHS

Not necessarily rights of way

M 1 or A 6(M)	Motorway
A 31(T)	Trunk road
A 35	Main road
B 3074	Secondary road
A 35	Dual carriageway
	Road generally more than 4m wide
	Road generally less than 4m wide
	Other road, drive or track

Unfenced roads and tracks are shown by pecked lines

.... Path

PUBLIC RIGHTS OF WAY

- - - - - - - Public paths { Footpath / Bridleway

–+–+–+–+ Road used as a public path

RAILWAYS

Multiple track	Standard gauge
Single track	
Narrow gauge	
Siding	
Cutting	
Embankment	
Tunnel	
Road over & under	
Level crossing, station	

BOUNDARIES

— · — · —	County (England and Wales) Region or Islands Area (Scotland)
— — — —	District
–·–·–·–	London Borough
·············	Civil Parish (England)* Community (Wales)
— — — —	Constituency (County, Borough or Burgh)

Coincident boundaries are shown by the first appropriate symbol opposite

*For Ordnance Survey purposes County Boundary is deemed to be the limit of the parish structure whether or not a parish area adjoins

1.1 Map Symbols

Symbols are used to show information on maps. Names and labels tell us a great deal, but there is so much information that some form of shorthand is needed. That is why symbols are used. Every type of map has its own set of symbols, and this includes the 'official' maps of Britain produced by the **Ordnance Survey** (O.S., for short). The most popular O.S. maps are in the Landranger Series and the more detailed Pathfinder Series. The symbols used for both sets of maps are given on pages 4 and 5. These questions are based on Map Extract 1.

1 Lerwick is the 'capital' of the Shetlands.
   (a) Which two main roads pass through the town?
   (*Hint: give their A-numbers*)
   (b) Which other type of important road also runs through Lerwick?
   (c) How can you tell that Lerwick is a busy port? Give at least three pieces of map evidence.
   (d) From where does the town get its supplies of electricity and drinking water?
   (e) Why are the oldest and busiest parts of Lerwick located around the Town Hall?
   (f) What services can Lerwick offer visiting tourists?

2 Scalloway is the Shetlands' 'second' town and once was its ancient capital. Look at the map extract.
   (a) Which building shows that Scalloway was important many centuries ago?
   (b) Which kinds of public building are found in Lerwick and Scalloway?
   (c) How do both ports provide a safe harbour for shipping? (*Hint: think of bad weather!*)
   (d) What is the highest spot height on any of the roads between the two towns?
   (e) Why do these roads curve so much?

3 What local words seem to mean:
   (a) a bay? (two possible answers)
   (b) a headland?
   (c) a lake?
   (d) a small island?
   (e) a stream?

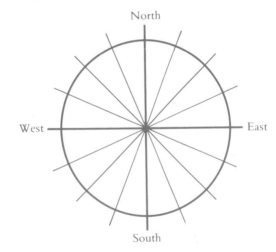

Fig. 1.2A The Compass Rose

The four main compass directions – north, south, east and west – are called **cardinal points**. The directions lying between them are the **intermediate points**. Both sets of directions can be shown on a **compass rose** (Fig. 1.2A). The intermediate points always take their names from the two directions they lie between, with north or south always coming first. For example: north-west lies between north and west. *Three*-word intermediate directions can begin with any of the four cardinal points. For example: east-south-east lies between east and south-east.

1 (a) Draw Fig. 1.2A then label all the notches on its outer edge with their correct intermediate points.
   (b) Write 'Cardinal Points' and 'Intermediate Points' on the appropriate lines in the key.

Compass directions on O.S. maps are based on Grid North – the vertical blue lines printed on these maps. All other directions can be worked out from these lines. Example: Trondra Island lies to the south-west of Scalloway.

2 Which compass rose directions would you use to go directly:
   (a) from Wester Quarff to Easter Quarff?
   (b) from Scalloway to the Ness of Burwick?
   (c) from Wester Quarff to Scalloway?
   (d) from Trondra Island to Lerwick?
   (e) from Lerwick to Scalloway?

Map Extract 1 : *Shetland Island, Scotland* 1:50 000 (1989)

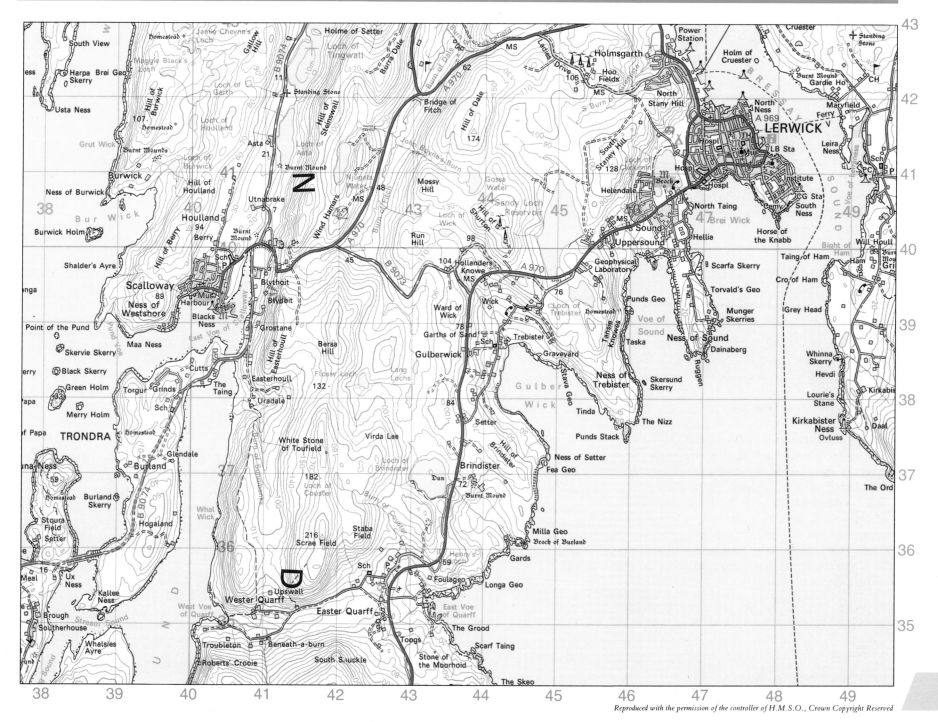

1.3 Scales and Distances

Scale is the link between real-life distances and those on a map. It can be shown in three ways:

- as a statement, for example: '1 cm stands for ½ km', which is the scale of the Landranger Series maps.
- as a ratio (also called the **Representative Fraction**), for example: '1:10 000', which means that the basic layout of the map is only 1/10 000th of its real-life size.
- as a **linear scale**, for example:

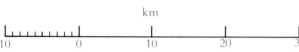

Note that the left part of the scale is sub-divided into smaller units. These make it easier to measure parts of a kilometre.

To measure the **direct** distance between two points, first mark both their positions on the edge of a piece of paper. Then place this edge under the linear scale and read off the correct number of whole and part kilometres. Measuring **indirect** routes takes a little longer, but the basic idea is the same. The trick is to choose a straight-edged piece of paper and adjust it at every bend along the route. This changes the indirect distance into a straight one, which can be measured on the linear scale in the usual way.

1 Use the linear scale shown above in this column, to measure (in km) each of the distances from A to B shown in the next column.

Questions 2 to 4 are based on Map Extract 1.

2 (a) What is the length (in cm) along the side of any grid square on this map extract?

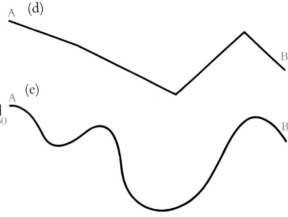

(b) How many km does this number of cm stand for?
(c) What, then, is the scale of this O.S. map? Write your answer as a statement.
(d) What is the real-life distance along the top of the map extract?
(e) What is the total area of the extract – measured in square kilometres?

3 Write down the direct distances (to the nearest 0.1 km) between:
(a) the northern and southern tips of Sandy Loch Reservoir.
(b) Burwick Holm and Merry Holm islands on the western side of the map.
(c) the Geophysical Laboratory south-west of Lerwick and the radio station north-west of the town.

(d) Lerwick Youth Hostel and the golf course at the Bridge of Fitch road junction on the A970.
(e) Scalloway Post Office and Lerwick Town Hall.

4 What are the road distances along these routes:
(a) the B9074 from its junction with the A970 to the top edge of the map?
(b) the road connecting the two Trondra bridges, from the centre-point of each bridge?
(c) Lerwick Hospital (the one on the A970) to Lerwick Cemetery – using only 'coloured' roads?
(d) Lerwick Town Hall to Scalloway Post Office, using the northern (A970) route?
(e) Lerwick Town Hall to Scalloway Post Office, via the southern (A970/B9073) route?

5 Draw an accurate plan of your own bedroom. Measure the walls first, then the sizes of the furniture. Don't forget the door and the window! Add a suitable linear scale and a compass will give you the direction of north, which can also be shown.

Fig. 1.3A The road to Trondra, Shetland Island

8

1.4 Grid References

O.S. maps are useful to many groups of people. Town planners study them before approving new roads and buildings, students need them for practical fieldwork exercises, and mountain rescue teams always carry them during emergencies. All have to pin-point map locations quickly and accurately, and can do this by means of a **grid reference** system covering the whole country. This appears on O.S. maps as a network of numbered lines printed in light blue. The north-south lines in this grid are called **eastings** because their numbers, which are shown along the top and bottom of a map, increase towards the east; the horizontal lines across a map are the **northings** – they increase towards the north. Fig. 1.4A explains how each grid line square can be given its own four-figure grid reference (G.R.) number. This type of reference is used to locate large features such as villages, woods and lakes. Note that:

- the easting number is taken before the northing – easy to remember as *E* comes before *N* in the alphabet.

- the lower grid line number is chosen in each case, i.e. the easting down the left side of the square and the northing along its bottom.

- both chosen grid lines cross at the bottom left hand corner of the square.

Smaller map features (e.g. buildings and road junctions) use the more accurate *six-*figure grid reference system. You have to imagine that each chosen square is sub-divided into 100 smaller squares (see Fig. 1.4B), then estimate how many tenths should be added to the easting and northing figures. Features actually on a grid line will have 'o' as the third or sixth number; those at a square

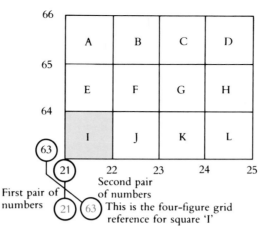

Fig. 1.4A *How to find the four-figure grid reference of a square*

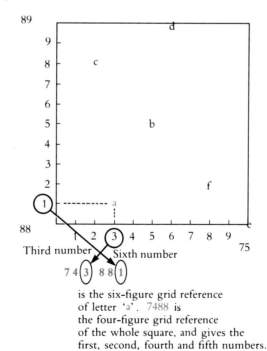

7 4 ③ 8 8 ① is the six-figure grid reference of letter 'a'. 7488 is the four-figure grid reference of the whole square, and gives the first, second, fourth and fifth numbers.

Fig. 1.4B *How to find a six-figure grid reference position*

corner will have a 'o' for both of these numbers.

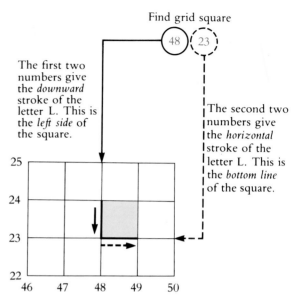

Fig. 1.4C *The 'L' method of using a four-figure grid reference to find a square*

Fig. 1.4C shows you how to do the opposite – to find map features from the grid reference positions you have been given.

1 (a) List at least five different groups of people who would use O.S. maps for work, education or pleasure. You can include the examples given in this unit.
(b) How are O.S. maps likely to help each of these groups of people?

2 Name the **lochs** or **islands** in Map Extract 1 within these grid reference squares: 3840, 4238, 4340, 4539 and 4742.

3 Pair up these grid reference positions in Extract 2 with their correct features:

241552	contour line
251527	rocks
257531	sand
258549	secondary road
261533	spot height

4 Write down the four-figure grid reference numbers of:

(a) squares A, F, H, J and L in Fig. 1.4A

(b) the squares in Map Extract 1 which contain these villages: Cutts, Easter Quarff, Gulberwick, Holmsgarth and Trebister

(c) the squares in Map Extract 2 containing these places: Plaidy, Hannafore, Trenant Wood, Portlooe and St. Martin

5 What are the six-figure grid references of letters b, c, d, e and f in Fig. 1.4B?

6 Give the six-figure grid reference positions of these features:

(a) in Map Extract 1:
– the road junction at Bridge of Fitch
– the island in the Loch of Brindister
– Scalloway Post Office
– the spot height at 45m on the B9073
– Lerwick Youth Hostel

(b) in Map Extract 2:
– Merrifields Farm buildings
– Inner Kimlers rocks
– St. Martin Church
– the highest point on Looe Island
– the quarry nearest to Trenant Park

7 Choose any five other features in Map Extract 2 which are likely to attract tourists to Looe and the surrounding area. For each one:

(a) name and describe the feature

(b) give its six-figure grid reference.

Map Extract 2: *Looe, 1:25 000 (1983)*

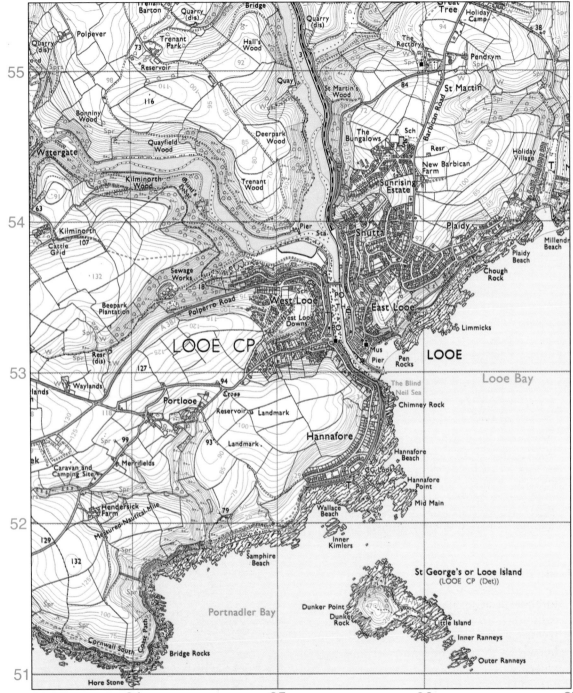

1.5 Route Planning

Orienteers and rally enthusiasts will already have some experience of using route directions. The aim is always to supply enough information for a person to follow a certain route, even if he or she is unfamiliar with the area it is in. Route planning uses all the basic mapwork skills introduced so far, and is best done by taking each 'leg' of the route separately. This example shows the kind of wording which may be used; it refers to the northern route between Lerwick and Scalloway on Map Extract 1.

'Start at Lerwick Lifeboat Station (GR479412) and travel north-westwards along the A969 main road. After going about 0.9 km along this road, ignore the left turning at GR473417 but keep to the right at the T-junction and join the A970 coastal main road. Then turn quickly left on to Ladies Drive until turning left again in square 4442 on to the A970. At Bridge of Fitch (GR 431420) take the left fork and continue mainly in a south-westerly direction for 4½ km; ignore the junctions with the B9073 and then the B9074 secondary roads, but take extra care down a steep hair-pin bend which is south-west of Wind Hamers. Scalloway Post Office is on the right side of the A970, just past the school, at GR403397'.

1 Write detailed route plans:
(a) from Scalloway Post Office to Lerwick Lifeboat Station (this is the opposite of the route described above)
(b) from Scalloway Post Office to the Lerwick camp site at GR466415 – using the *southerly* (A970/B9073) route

2 Work in pairs for this exercise, which can be based on any 1:50 000 or 1:25 000 scale map in this book.
(a) Each member of your pair writes one set of route directions. You then exchange and follow them carefully. Finally, discuss between yourselves any problems you met while doing this. Try to think of ways of improving the directions to avoid similar problems in the future.
(b) Describe what you would expect to see along each side of your chosen route.

3 Using the techniques you perfected in question 2, do a similar exercise based on your local area. It is a good idea to choose a different scale (eg 1:2500 or 1:10560) of Ordnance Survey map to the one you used for the last question.

Fig. 1.5A A group of young walkers

Fig. 1.5B Using a map

1.6 Natural Landscape Features

Relief describes the physical nature of the land surface. Its height can be shown on maps as spot heights or contours. Only contour patterns, however, can reveal the shape of the surface.

1 (a) What is the height difference (in metres) between the contour lines on Landranger 1:50 000 scale maps? (see Map Extract 1).
(b) What is the height difference between the *darker* coloured contour lines on this scale of map?
(c) Repeat (a) and (b) for Pathfinder 1:25 000 scale maps like the one in Map Extract 2.

1

2

3

4

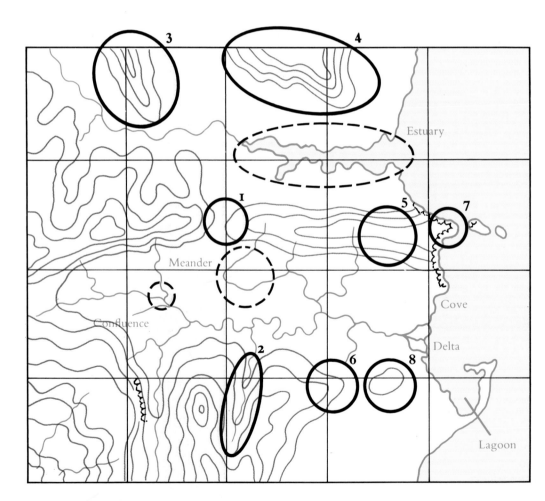

5

6

7

8

(d) State at least one *natural* and one *artificial* map feature where spot heights are often printed. You can use any extracts in this book to find this information.

2 This question is based on the eight photographs in Fig. 1.6A. For each photograph:
(a) write down its number
(b) name and describe the physical feature shown in it (use the entries in the table below)
(c) briefly describe the contour pattern of each feature. *Your teacher may also tell you to draw the pattern – to help you to remember it.*

Type of relief feature	Description of feature
Knoll	small isolated hill
Plateau	flat-topped area of high land
Spur	finger of high land which jutts out into an area of lower land
Ridge	long narrow area of higher land
Cuesta	ridge with one side much steeper than the other (also called an **escarpment**)
Cliff	very high steep slope
Valley	narrow area of lowland which has higher land on both sides. Valleys are widest at their lower end and usually contain a river.
Pass	long valley providing a natural routeway across an upland area (also called a **gap**).

3 Six natural water features have been named in Fig. 1.6A. Copy their names then write down your own descriptions of these features.

Fig. 1.6A A Types of relief feature, contour patterns and water features

13

1.7 Slopes and Cross-sections

Contour patterns may be used to study height changes along a straight line. Diagrams which display this kind of information are called **cross-sections**. The examples in Figs. 1.7A–C are based on types of slope often shown on O.S. maps.

1 For each slope in Figs. 1.7A–C:
   (a) name the type of slope
   (b) draw its contour plan
   (c) describe carefully how the slope changes *as the height increases*

2 Identify the type of slope between:
   (a) points A and B, C and D, and E and F in Fig. 1.7F
   (b) these positions on Map Extract 2:
      – GR264545 and GR269547
      – GR250525 and GR250523
      – GR237516 and GR239514

Fig. 1.7A *An even slope*

Fig. 1.7B *A concave slope*

Fig. 1.7C *A convex slope*

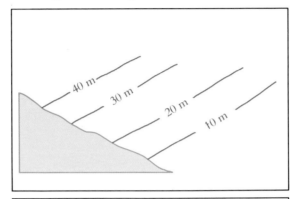

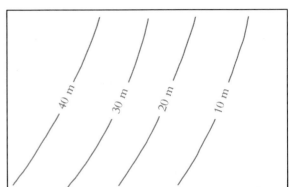

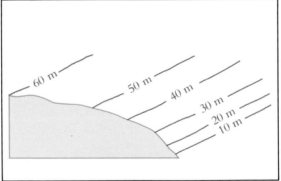

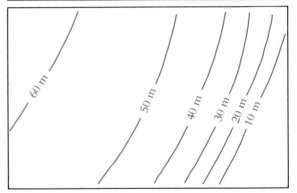

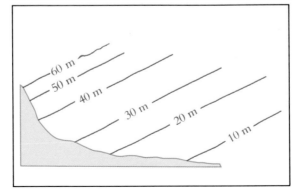

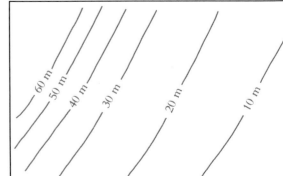

14

Stage 1

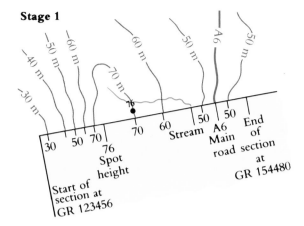

Stage 2

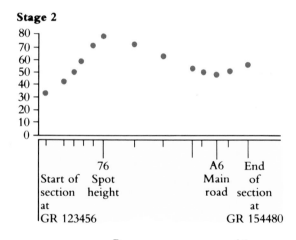

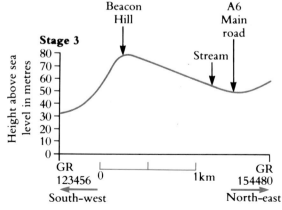

Fig. 1.7D *How to draw a relief cross-section*

STAGE ONE

- Find the section's start and end positions on the map.

- Place a straight-edged piece of paper under the section line as shown. The left corner of the edge should be under the start position.

- Put on the piece of paper all the information you will need to draw the section. The positions and heights of the contour lines are very important.

STAGE TWO

- Draw the horizontal and vertical axis lines. Mark off and label the height intervals up the vertical axis.

- Place the piece of paper under the horizontal axis, then put a small mark above the position of every contour line and spot height. The vertical scale shows you how far up the graph each mark should be.

STAGE THREE

- Join the height dots together with a smooth line.

- Use arrows to label the positions of the features you noted down on the piece of paper.

- Add:
  (a) a label for the height scale
  (b) grid reference positions of the start and end positions
  (c) two compass direction arrows for the cross-section line
  (d) a linear scale
  (e) a title

Fig. 1.7D shows you how to draw and then complete a relief cross-section. Note that:

- the section line is smooth; it doesn't have sharp angles because these rarely occur in nature.
- the tops and bottoms of the slopes are not cut off – they need to be rounded, for the same reason as given above.
- the spot height on Beacon Hill has been used to draw a more accurate cross-section.
- the height scale has been chosen so as to produce a realistic cross-section. Exaggerating the height scale too much makes quite gentle slopes look like steep mountainsides!
- labels are added to highlight the most important natural and human features along the section.

3 Study the *very* poor example of a relief cross-section in Fig. 1.7E, then note down any changes or additions you would make to it.

Fig. 1.7E *Cross-section for question 3*

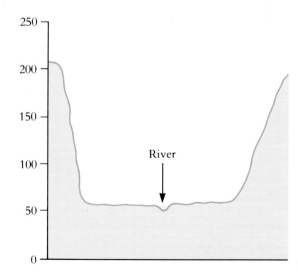

4 (a) Draw a relief cross-section from Point G to Point H on Fig. 1.7F.

(b) Describe how the land surface changes along this section from left to right. Use the three slope terms in Figs. 1.7A–C whenever necessary.

(c) Draw a fully labelled relief cross-section from GR250530 to GR250520 on Map Extract 2.

(d) Draw a third cross-section from GR400370 to GR450370 on Map Extract 1.

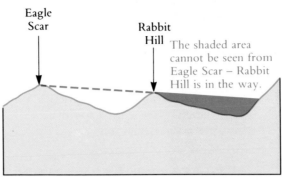

Fig. 1.7G *Using a cross-section to work out the intervisibility of two places*

Intervisibility

Cross-sections provide one way of working out the **intervisibility** between places on a map (Fig. 1.7G). This tells you whether or not they can be seen from each other.

5 Using the cross-section you drew for question 4(d), discover whether the places in each pair of grid references can be seen directly from each other.

(a) GR410370 and GR400370

(b) GR420370 and GR430370

(c) GR430370 and GR440370

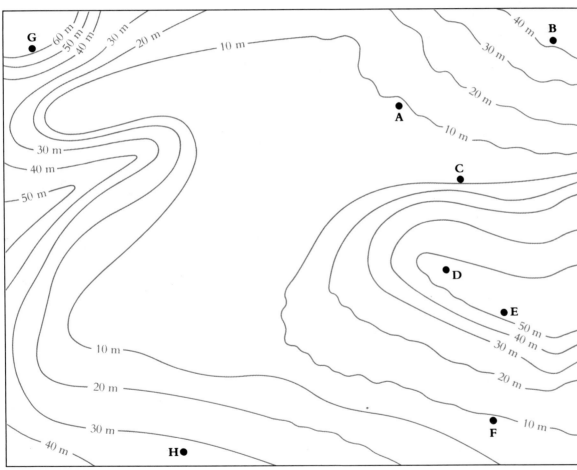

Fig. 1.7F *Map for questions 2(a) and 3(a)*

Fig. 1.7H *Photograph to show intervisibility*

1.8 Links with Photographs

Maps help us to build up mental pictures of what their areas look like. These can never be as accurate as photographs, of course, but even they are of little value unless you have some idea of (a) the direction the camera was facing and (b) where the picture was taken from.

To find (a) and (b), begin by locating one important feature (e.g. a pier, quarry or church) on both the photograph and the map.

Then do the same with other features until you are fairly sure of the camera's direction and position.

1 Answer these questions for the photographs in Figs. 1.8A and B.
(a) Name (or describe clearly) features A–E.
(b) In which compass direction was the camera pointing?
(c) Say where the camera would have been when the photograph was taken. You can give a four-figure grid reference or a general description such as 'To the south-west of . . .'.

2 State the ways in which the two areas in these photographs are
(a) similar
(b) different.
You could consider relief, the urban areas and the countryside areas. It is best to study each point separately.

Fig. 1.8A Aerial photograph of part of the Map Extract 1 area

Fig. 1.8B Aerial photograph of part of Map Extract 2 area

2.1 Glaciated Highlands

Water movements are responsible for many changes in the world's natural landscapes. Just a few examples are: rain falling on bare soil, ice in valley glaciers, strong river currents and waves pounding on a beach. Each movement re-arranges the soil, sand etc on the surface, and this happens in three ways:

Erosion – the loosening and wearing away of fixed material
Transportation – the carrying of the eroded material from one place to another

Helvellyn is one of the highest of the Cumbrian Mountains and lies at the heart of the English Lake District. Its main rocks are volcanic ash and solidified lava, and these give Helvellyn and other nearby mountains their rugged, interesting outlines. Both rock-types are ancient and very hard, but were seriously eroded by the constant movement of ice.

Some of the surface rock was eroded by the weight of the ice sheets which were several hundred metres deep in parts. Also, the ice would freeze solid around any pieces of rock sticking out from the mountainside then 'pluck' them out as it moved slowly downhill. These jagged pieces became embedded in the ice and gave it extra cutting power. Erosion caused by rock fragments rather than the ice itself is called **abrasion**.

Deposition – the 'dropping' of the material after it has been transported

Units 2.1–2.4 show all three processes in action.

The Ice Age lasted one million years, but ended only 12 000 years ago. In geological (rock-history) terms, a few thousand years is a very short period of time. This means that the effects of ice on the landscape are still quite easy to see.

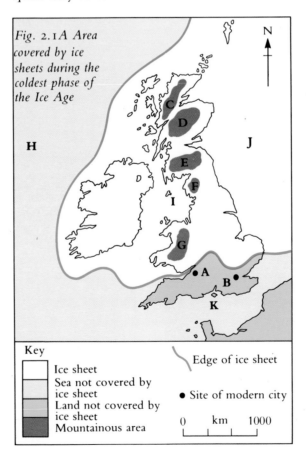

Fig. 2.1A Area covered by ice sheets during the coldest phase of the Ice Age

Key
Ice sheet
Sea not covered by ice sheet
Land not covered by ice sheet
Mountainous area

Edge of ice sheet

● Site of modern city

0   km   1000

Fig. 2.1B Stages in the glaciation of an upland area

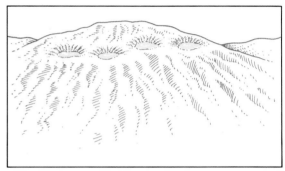

Stage 1: Hollows are filled with snow and ice

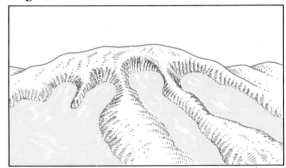

Stage 2: Hollows being deepened into cirques (also called corries). Tongues of ice flow from the hollows into the valleys below

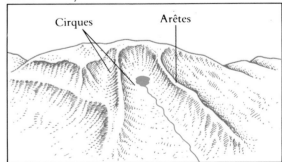

Stage 3: After the Ice Age: cirques are separated by sharp ridges called arêtes

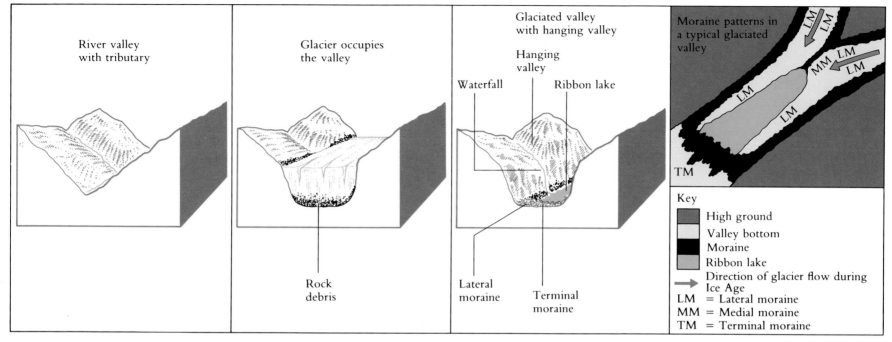

River valley with tributary

Glacier occupies the valley

Rock debris

Glaciated valley with hanging valley

Hanging valley

Waterfall   Ribbon lake

Lateral moraine   Terminal moraine

Moraine patterns in a typical glaciated valley

LM

MM LM

LM

LM

LM

TM

Key

High ground
Valley bottom
Moraine
Ribbon lake
Direction of glacier flow during Ice Age
LM = Lateral moraine
MM = Medial moraine
TM = Terminal moraine

Fig. 2.1C Stages in the glaciation of a river valley

Fig. 2.1B shows three stages in the glaciation of upland areas like the Lake District. Snow first collected in sheltered hollows near the summits, where the air was coldest. The weight of this snow compressed it into hard ice. This enlarged and deepened the hollows so that they now appear as huge basins (**cirques/corries/cwms**) carved out of the mountainside; lakes now often lie inside their over-deepened bottoms. The outer edges of adjoining cirques cut back towards each other until only narrow ridges (**arêtes**) separated them.

The cirques acted as gathering grounds for the ice. This spilled out and into the valleys below where it formed **glaciers** – rivers of solid ice. Fig. 2.1C shows how glaciers altered the size and shape of existing river valleys. It also points out where the glaciers deposited **moraines** made up of the material they had transported. **Terminal moraines** have often acted as natural dams across valleys. These have trapped river water and created long, narrow **ribbon (finger) lakes** behind them. Many of Cumbria's lakes were formed in this way.

Fig. 2.1D Photograph for question 4

19

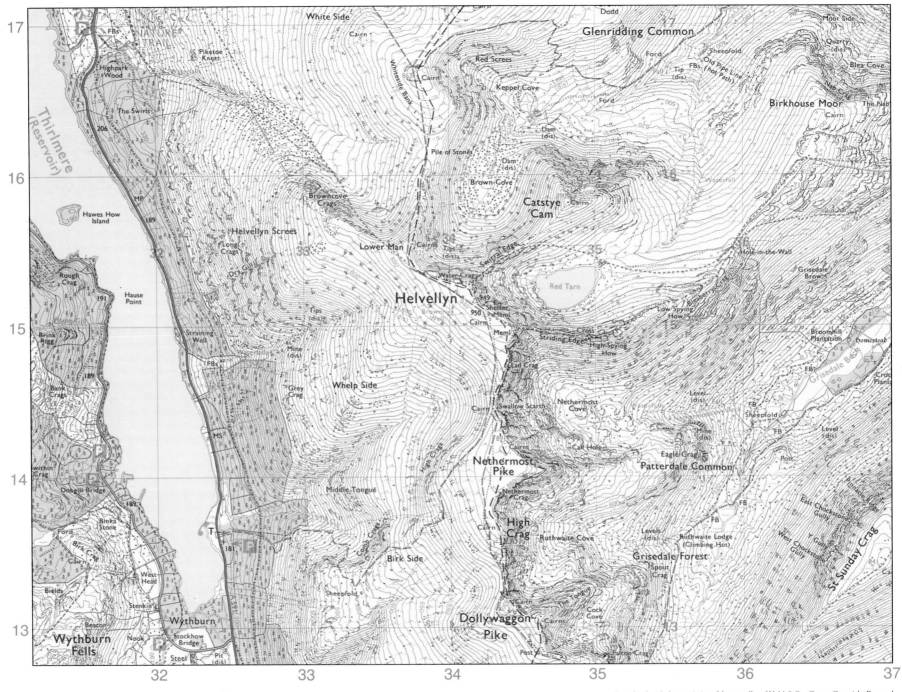

Thirlmere (Reservoir)

White Side

Glenridding Common

Dodd

Moor Side

Quarry (dis)

Sheepfold

FBs

Old Pipe Line (not Path)

Blea Cove

Nab Crag

The Nab

Birkhouse Moor

Cairn

Piketoe Knott

Highpark Wood

The Swirls

206

189

MP

Hawes How Island

Rough Crag

191

Hause Point

Brink Rigg

189

Bank Crags

Straining Well

FBs

MS

Dobgill Bridge

189

Binka Stone

Ford

Birk Crag

Cairn

West Head

Bields

Stenkin

Beacon

Wythburn

Nook

Stockhow Bridge

Steel

Pit (dis)

Wythburn Fells

Red Screes

Keppel Cove

Ford

Ford

Dam (dis)

Whiteside Bank

Cairn

Pile of Stones

Dam (dis)

Browncove Crags

Brown Cove

Catstye Cam

Cairn

Helvellyn Screes

Long Crags

Gill

Lower Man

Cairns

Tips (dis)

Swirral Edge

Water Crag

Red Tarn

Grisedale Brow

Hole-in-the-Wall

Helvellyn

Shelter Mem'l

950

Cairn

Mem'l

Low Spying How

Cross

Striding Edge

High Spying How

Broomhill Plantation

Homestead

Tips (dis)

Mine (dis)

Grey Crag

Whelp Side

Lad Crag

Swallow Scarth

Nethermost Cove

Level (dis)

Grisedale Beck

Cross Plant

FB

Cairn

Cairns

Calf Hole

Nethermost Pike

Eagle Crag

Patterdale Common

Post

FB

High Crags

Middle Tongue

Nethermost Crag

Mine (dis)

Level (dis)

FB

High Crag

Cairn

Ruthwaite Cove

Levels (dis)

Ruthwaite Lodge (Climbing Hut)

FB

East Chockstone Gully

Cobb Crags

Birk Side

Sheepfold

Grisedale Forest

Spout Crag

West Chockstone Gully

St Sunday Crag

Dollywaggon Pike

Cairns

The Tongue

Cock Cove

Post

Falcon Crag

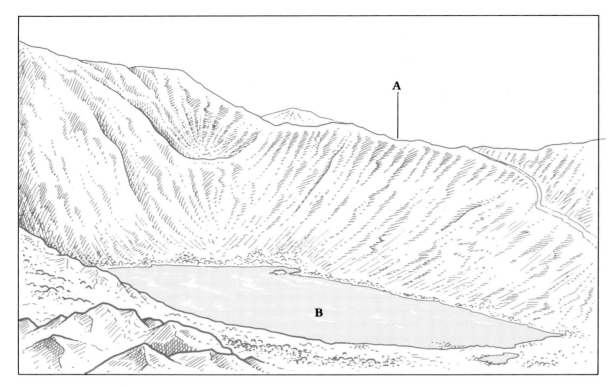

Fig. 2.1E Diagram for question 4(a)

1 (a) Draw Fig. 2.1A onto an outline map of the British Isles, but don't copy the letters printed on it.
(b) On your map, name:
cities A and B
upland areas C–G
sea areas H–K

2 With the help of your completed map:
(a) describe the southern limit of the ice.
(b) explain why the south coast of England was not covered by the ice.

Map Extract 3 : *Helvellyn*, 1:25 000 (1988)

3 Pair up these terms with their correct descriptions: *lateral moraine, medial moraine, terminal moraine*
. . . was formed across the lower end of a glaciated valley, where the slightly warmer air melted the glacier's snout (leading edge).
. . . was formed along the valley sides, after surface material had fallen from the bare rock faces higher up.
. . . was formed where two lateral moraines joined.

4 (a) Copy the line drawing, Fig. 2.1E, which is based on the photograph in Fig. 2.1D.
(b) State whether this picture was most probably taken from GR347150, GR347155 or GR351152 on Map Extract 3.
(c) Label glaciated features A and B.

(d) Describe how these two features were formed by ice action.

5 Explain why:
(a) a glacier at GR356156 would have flowed in a north-easterly direction.
(b) most of Thirlmere's eastern shore is quite straight.
(c) this shore bulges outwards into the lake at GR323137. (*Hint: think about the stream which enters the lake there*).
(d) there are large forests around Thirlmere, but none by Red Tarn. Consider human activity as well as natural reasons.

6 You wish to park your car in a convenient place then walk to the summit of Helvellyn – but using only the public footpaths shown in Map Extract 3. These extra 1:25 000 scale map symbols will help you to answer the questions which follow.

	Boundary of National Park Access Land
	Access Land is National Park Planning Board land which is open to the public

PUBLIC RIGHTS OF WAY

		Footpath
- - - - - - -	Public Paths	
— — — —		Bridleway
—·—·—·—·—	Road used as a public path	

Fig. 2.1F OS symbols for public paths

Reproduced with the permission of the controller of H.M.S.O., Crown Copyright Reserved

(a) State where you would park your car.
(b) Describe the route you would take to reach the summit.
(c) Give full reasons for choosing this route. Consider distance and gradient in your answer.

7 (a) What problems are large numbers of hikers likely to cause on mountainsides?
(b) Suggest practical ways of reducing these problems.

2.2 Carboniferous Limestone Scenery

There are two types of limestone rock. **Jurassic** limestone is soft and porous, and is common in the south and east of England. **Carboniferous** limestone is twice as old (about 250 million years), much harder, and forms large upland areas further north. This case study is based on the slopes of Ingleborough Hill, one of England's highest and most interesting mountains. Fig. 2.2A shows its position and the relief of the surrounding area.

Carboniferous limestone scenery has a number of features which make it easy to recognise:

- **scars** – long, steep cliffs of bare rock. They follow the valley sides and may be

Fig. 2.2B(i) Limestone scars (general view)

Fig. 2.2B(ii) Limestone scars (close-up)

'stepped' at different levels (Fig. 2.2B(i)).
- a rock structure similar to that of a brick wall. The long, horizontal lines in the 'brick' pattern are **bedding planes**. These formed as layers of material were being deposited on the sea bed and later compressed into solid rock. The vertical lines, which are much shorter, are called **joints**. These lines of weakness have been caused by the rock layers drying out and then contracting. This happened after they had been forced upwards above sea level and created new land.
- **limestone pavement** – a flat, bare area of rock which is being weathered by rain and carbon dioxide gas. This chemical formula shows what happens:

$$H_2O + CO_2 + CaCO_3 = Ca(HCO_3)_2$$

H_2O is rain water.
CO_2 is the carbon dioxide gas in the air. This dissolves in the rainwater and turns it into weak carbonic acid.
$CaCO_3$ is calcium carbonate (the limestone). This is insoluble in water.
$Ca(HCO_3)_2$ is calcium bicarbonate, formed when the carbonic acid acts on the limestone and makes it soluble.

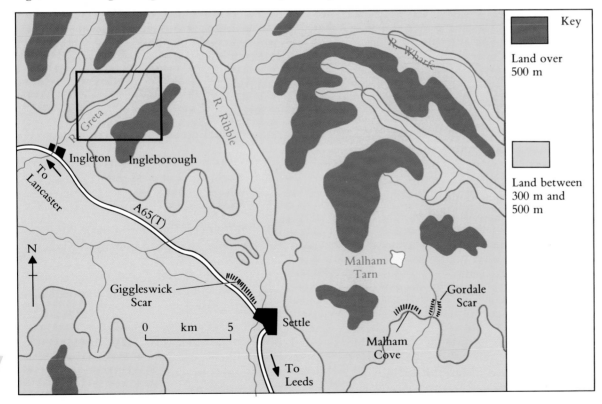

Fig. 2.2A The Ingleborough area

The acidic rainwater attacks all the exposed parts of the limestone, but has the greatest effect on the lines of weakness – that is down the joints and along the bedding planes. The result is a 'bar-of-chocolate' shaped-surface, with rows of blocks called **clints**. These are separated by steep-sided **grykes** which may be several metres deep (Fig. 2.2C).

- lack of surface drainage. Carboniferous limestone is **permeable**. This means that water can seep through it along the bedding planes and down the joints, but not through the more solid rock between them. On its journey below ground the carbonic acid rainwater dissolves the limestone and transports it elsewhere. This creates underground passages and caves. Clusters of 'pots' and 'caves' on O.S. maps are a sure sign of Carboniferous limestone country. There are many examples of both in the Ingleborough area (e.g. White Scar Cave at GR713745 on Map Extract 4).
- **swallow holes**, down which surface streams flow underground after passing over an area of impermeable rock. They later emerge as **springs**. Lines of swallow holes and springs can, therefore, show where and how the surface rock changes.

Fig. 2.2C Limestone pavement. General view (inset) and close up

RUNNEL

CLINT BLOCK

GRYKE

The area in Map Extract 4 has wide, sweeping valleys and the towering bulk of Ingleborough Hill is never far away. Some of its best limestone features are on a shelf lying between the mountain and the valley of the River Greta (also called Chapel Beck!) The soils on this shelf are thin and **acidic** and very infertile and the solid rock often outcrops through its poor pasture. Sheep-grazing is the main activity there.

The Greta Valley became much larger during the Ice Age. It was widened and deepened by a glacier and this erosion helped to create Twisleton and Raven Scars. The river's vertical (downwards) erosion has since exposed lower and much older impermeable rocks such as slate. The valley bottom now has a thin surface layer of clay. As this is also impermeable, it too can support a small river. The village of Chapel-le-Dale, the main roads and a number of farm houses are located within this valley.

The cross-section in Fig. 2.2D shows that Ingleborough Hill is also made up of different rock layers, some of them much harder than others. The hardest one of all is millstone grit, another common rock in the Pennines. It forms a protective 'cap' on the top of the mountain, and has given it a plateau summit instead of a sharp peak. The now ruined fort on the summit was built by a tribe of Ancient Britons called the Brigantes. Lower down are the Yoredale Series rocks. Fig. 2.2B explains the link between these layers and the mountain's curious, uneven outline.

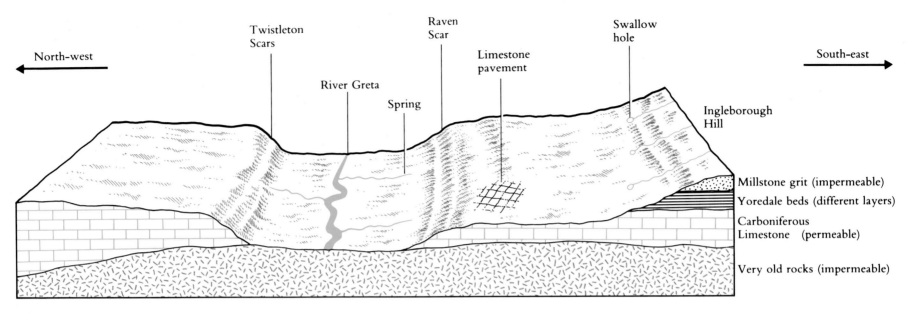

North-west ← ... → South-east

Twistleton Scars
Raven Scar
Swallow hole
Limestone pavement
River Greta
Spring
Ingleborough Hill

Millstone grit (impermeable)
Yoredale beds (different layers)
Carboniferous Limestone (permeable)
Very old rocks (impermeable)

Fig. 2.2D Section across the Greta Valley

1 Which Carboniferous limestone features are found at: GR713745, GR724750, GR725742, GR744767, GR748759 and GR748764? (*Hint: one of them is a limestone pavement*).

2 (a) Make a simple line drawing of the scene in Fig. 2.2B(ii).
(b) Add labels to highlight the main limestone scenery features in this view.

3 Answer these questions about Mere Gill and its tributary streams:
(a) In which general compass direction does Mere Gill flow?
(b) At what height and 6-figure G.R. position is Mere Gill Hole?
(c) What happens to the stream at this point?
(d) What does this fact tell you about the change in surface rock there?
(e) Mere Gill is fed by six springs lying between the 450 and 650 metre (darker)
contour lines. Write down, as accurately as you can, the height of each of these springs. Then work out their average height. A magnifying glass can be used for this question.
(f) What does this information tell you about the surface rocks along that particular stretch of mountainside?

4 (a) Draw a relief cross-section along a straight line between GR720770 and the summit of Ingleborough Hill. You need only use the darker contours at 50 metre intervals.
(b) Locate and name these features on the cross-section: River Greta, Raven Scar, Twistleton Scars, Summit of Ingleborough Hill (plus its height), the chief road along each side of the valley.
(c) Label the start and finish of the section with their 6-figure grid reference positions.
(d) Add two arrows labelled 'North-west' and 'South-east' to show the compass directions along the section.

5 With the help of your completed cross-section and the other information given in this unit:
(a) Write down the approximate heights at which the two valley roads have been built.
(b) Describe their general positions within the valley.
(c) Explain why these heights and positions were chosen for the lines of the roads.
(d) This valley cross-section is symmetrical (has a similar shape on both sides). Suggest reasons why the valley has this particular shape.

6 Say whether the following statements appear to be true or false. Give full reasons for your answers.
(a) The fields in the Greta Valley are much smaller than those on higher land.
(b) Many of the smaller streams follow a reasonably straight course, but the River Greta does not.
(c) Chapel-le-Dale has been built at the most suitable place in the valley.

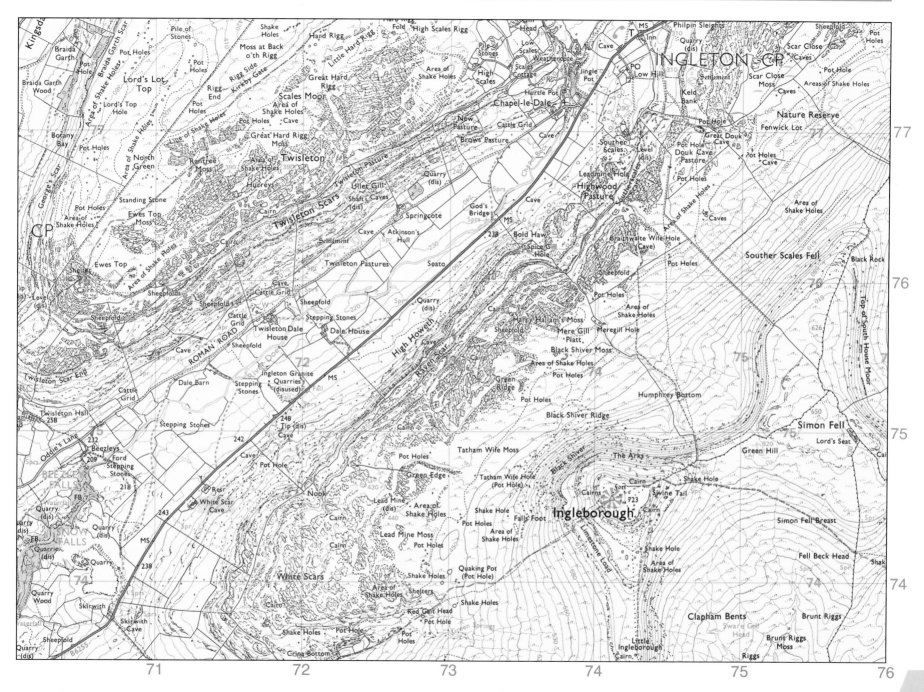

Map Extract 4 : *Ingleborough*, 1:25 000 (1988) *(River Doe is known locally as River Greta)*

2.3 River Valleys

Rain is often heaviest in upland areas. Soaked by frequent rainfall, upland soils act as a giant sponge and create tiny **rivulets** which later join to form streams. These can transport small pieces of peat and clay, but don't have enough energy to erode deep into the ground. That is why they are said to be at the **pre-valley** (or mountain) **stage**.

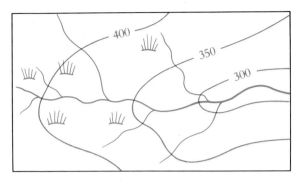

Fig. 2.3A The pre-valley stage

At the **upper valley stage**, the force of stream water can erode quite large pieces of rock. This process is called **hydraulic action**. The loosened pieces are transported by the rushing water, greatly increasing its cutting power. This effect is called **abrasion**. Where the stream bed is uneven, both water and material are swept around in whirlpools. They erode smooth, saucer-shaped hollows called **pot-holes**. After many years, these

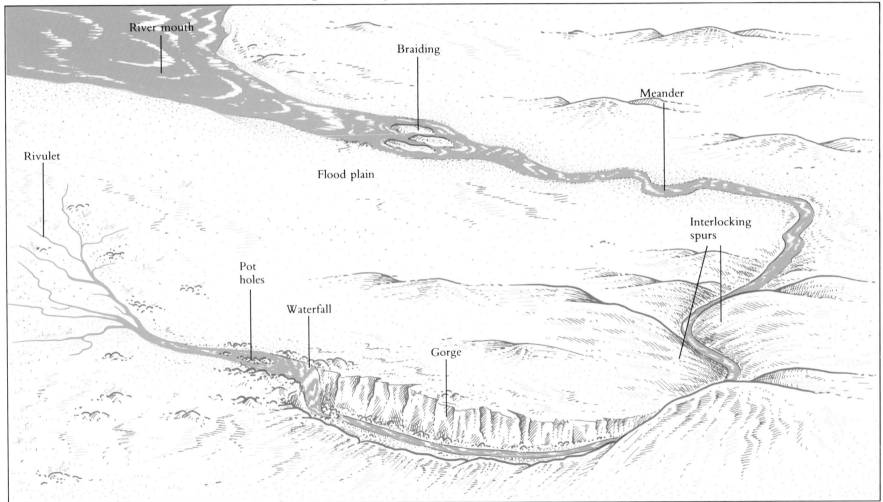

Fig. 2.3B The four river valley stages

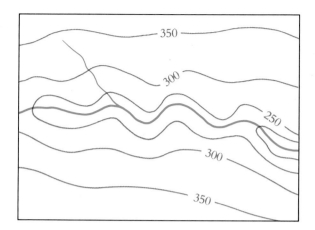

Fig. 2.3C The upper valley stage

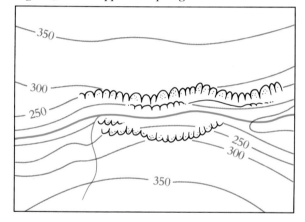

Fig. 2.3D The middle valley stage

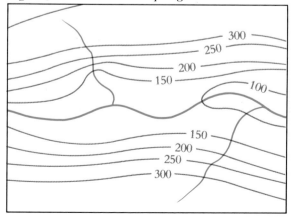

Fig. 2.3E The lower valley stage

hollows meet, lower the stream bed and produce valleys with a V–shaped contour pattern. Their vertical erosion may be powerful enough to cut narrow, steep-sided **gorges** and these often contain waterfalls.

The **middle valley stage** is further downstream, where the water flows much more slowly. Erosion of the river bed still takes place, but more of the river's energy is spent attacking the banks instead – by **lateral** (sideways) **erosion**. The river **meanders** as it flows between the **interlocking spurs** on either bank. The meanders become larger, the spurs are eroded further, widening and straightening the valley.

By the **lower valley stage**, the valley bottom is broader and flatter. The edges of the river's **flood plain** are steeper, and marked by the bunching of contours close together. The river meanders are much broader. Some deposition may take place in mid-stream and form long, low-lying islands, a process known as **braiding**.

1 (a) Write down the definitions of *erosion, transportation, hydraulic action, lateral erosion, pot-hole* (on a river bed, not in caving country!), and *vertical erosion*.

2 Explain why:
(a) Deposition is more important than erosion at the lower valley stage, but the opposite is true of the upper stage.
(b) Vertical erosion is most important at the upper valley stage.
(c) Lateral erosion is the main type of erosion further along a river's course.
(d) Braiding is most likely to occur at the lower valley stage.

3 Use the information in Figs. 2.3A–E to complete an enlarged copy of the table below.

Information	Valley stage		
	Upper	Middle	Lower
Steepness of valley sides★			
Width of valley bottom★			
Course of river			
General river features			

★ Use phrases such as 'very wide' and 'gentle gradient'

Fig. 2.3F A river meander

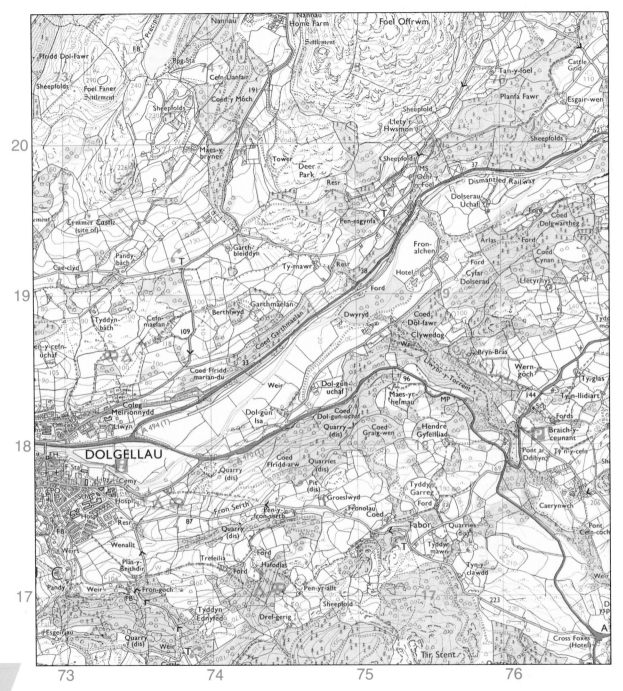

These questions are based on Map Extract 5.

4 At which stage is:
(a) the Afon Wnion in square 7418?
(b) the river by Torrent Walk in square 7518?
(c) the Nant Lwyd in square 7317?
(d) the network of streams around GR752178?

5 (a) Give 6 figure grid references for these features: a narrow gorge, part of a flood plain, a weir, the confluence of two rivers and the centre of a meander.
(b) Which one of the features in (a) is not natural?
(c) Discover for yourself why this kind of feature was built.

6 After class discussion, suggest reasons for the *shape* of the valley in the photo below.

Fig. 2.3G A mature river valley

28

Map Extract 5 : *Dolgellau*, 1:25 000 (1987)

2.4 Coastal Features

Landscape changes are probably most striking along the coast. This is especially true of west-facing shores which are open to the full force of Atlantic gales. This unit studies the main features of coastal erosion, transportation and deposition in turn.

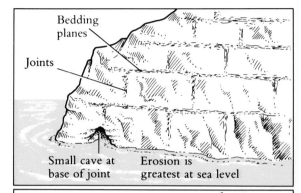

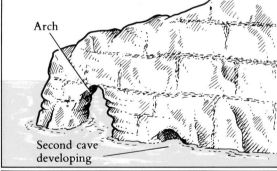

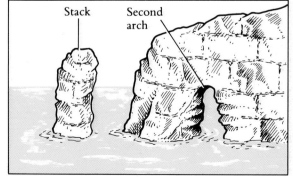

Fig. 2.4A Stages in the erosion of a headland

Headland erosion

Fig. 2.4A shows a typical headland, and the way it is most likely to be changed by erosion. Although very solid-looking, it is in fact riddled with lines of weakness. The sea attacks these joints and bedding planes, particularly those at the base of the cliff. Hydraulic action and abrasion open them up and slowly enlarge them into **caves**. Where major faults pass right through a headland, the caves formed at both sides eventually meet and create an **arch**. Further erosion – and the collapse of the central part of the arch – leaves a **stack**. The stack erodes down into a **stump** and then a **reef**, a low-lying shelf of rock. At the final stage, the reef is replaced by a **wave-cut platform** (beach) of sand or shingle. The whole process is constantly being repeated, causing the shoreline to retreat.

Fig. 2.4B A groyne on a beach

Longshore drift

Material eroded by the sea is constantly being transported along the coast. This movement is called **longshore drift**, and Fig. 2.4C explains why it takes place. It also shows how the directions of the **prevailing** (almost constant) **wind**, the offshore current, and the movement of beach material are all linked. Longshore drift is the cause of many problems, and lines of **groynes** built to reduce it are a common sight on British beaches (Fig. 2.4B).

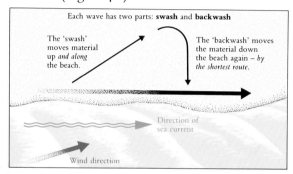

Fig. 2.4C Longshore drift

Deposition

Unit 2.3 showed that it is the slowing down of water which helps deposition to take place. In coastal areas, this often happens after the seawater has flowed around a headland and into the next bay. The result is a 'tail' of deposited material on the bottom which gradually builds up until it reaches the surface. The shape of the **spit** produced depends on the main wind and sea current directions. The curious finger-like **laterals** along it are caused by storms from other directions. The water in the **lagoon** is sheltered by both headland and spit; fine material transported by streams flowing into it speeds up the rate of deposition there. 'New' lagoon land is marshy but provides useful grazing for sheep.

1 (a) Explain why some parts of a headland are eroded more quickly than others.
(b) Make a copy of Fig. 2.4A then number the labelled features to show the order in which they are formed (e.g. joints and bedding planes are both at 'Stage 1').
(c) Write a sentence or two to show that each of these features is caused by coastal erosion: *arch, cave, reef, stack, wave-cut notch, wave-cut platform.*

2 State:
(a) what causes longshore drift to take place.
(b) how its effects may be reduced.

Questions based on Map Extract 6

3 Suggest possible reasons why:
(a) there is a headland at GR390951
(b) there is a bay (Porth Wen) in square 4094

(c) there is a fairly wide beach at the head of this bay

Fig. 2.4D An arch and a stack formed by coastal erosion

4 How can you tell that the stretch of coastline shown on Map Extract 6 has some very attractive scenery?

5 (a) Give the grid reference of the building shown in Fig. 2.4E and on Map Extract 6
(b) After class discussion, give reasons for the location of this nuclear power station.
Fig. 2.4E Wylfa Power Station

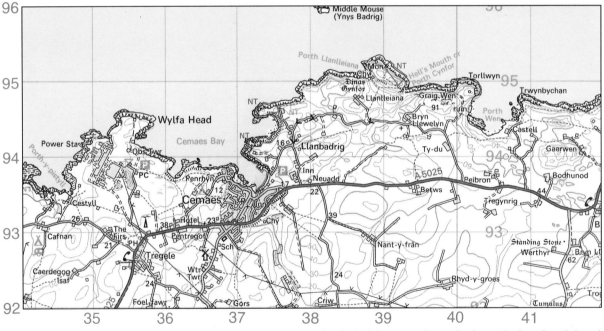

Map Extract 6 : *Anglesey*, 1:50 000 (1988)

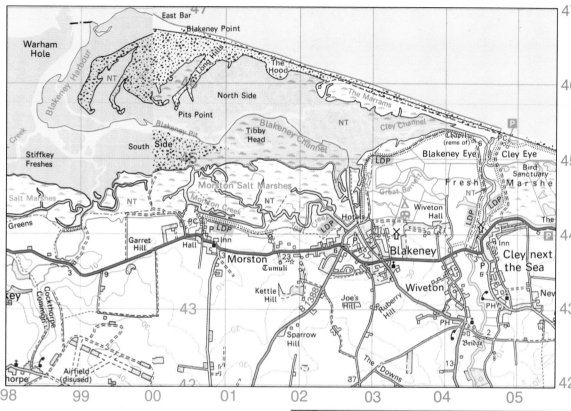

Map Extract 7 : *Blakeney*, 1:50 000 (1989)

8 Suggest reasons why an airfield was sited in the south-western corner of Map Extract 7. (*Hints: consider relief and population density; you may assume it was used by the RAF during the Second World War*).

9 Suggest ways in which the coastal spits in Map Extract 7 and Fig. 2.4F are:
(a) similar
(b) different

Fig. 2.4F Coastal spit

Questions based on Map Extract 7

6 (a) Does the main sea current along this stretch of coast flow from the east or the west? How can you tell?
(b) In which direction is the spit growing?
(c) What is particularly attractive about the coastal area shown in this extract? (At least three different ideas are needed).
(d) Where does most of the silt deposited in the Clay Channel come from?
(e) Why is the name of the village around GR045440 no longer as fitting as it used to be?

7 Make a simple line map of the map extract area, then label the main *natural* features within it.

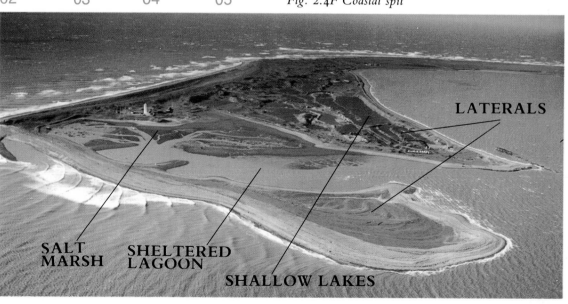

2.5 Settlement Patterns

Settlements are built-up areas. No two settlements are exactly alike, but many do have certain features in common. One of them is **site** – the place where a settlement first started to grow. Fig. 2.5A shows the most common types of village site. Another feature is **layout** which is the distribution and spacing of buildings within a community. The most usual types of layout are:

- **nucleated** – settlements which are compact and generally rounded in shape.
- **linear nucleated** – which are long and narrow. Their buildings are often strung out along a main road, river bank or shoreline.
- **dispersed** – countryside with scattered hamlets (small villages) or farms.

1 Complete the table below by putting one or more ticks on each line. The second column shows you which map extract to turn to.

2 (a) Which villages in Question 1 are (i) nucleated (ii) linear nucleated in shape?
(b) Explain why any one of these nucleated villages has this type of shape. Quote map evidence (e.g. about the relief of the land) in your answer.
(c) Do the same for one of the linear nucleated villages in (a).

3 Why do these grid squares have dispersed settlement layouts:

2352 in Map Extract 2 on page 10
3213 in Map Extract 3 on page 20
5802 in Map Extract 9 on page 39
5234 in Map Extract 12 on page 51
4306 in Map Extract 13a on page 54

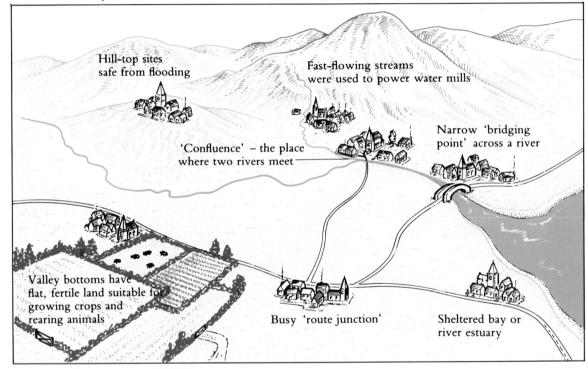

Fig. 2.5A Village sites

Hill-top sites safe from flooding

Fast-flowing streams were used to power water mills

Narrow 'bridging point' across a river

'Confluence' – the place where two rivers meet

Valley bottoms have flat, fertile land suitable for growing crops and rearing animals

Busy 'route junction'

Sheltered bay or river estuary

Name of Village	On Page	Site characteristic(s) of village								
		River bridging point	River confluence	Good defensive position	Route junction	On sheltered coast	On a river bank	Near entrance to valley	On reasonably flat land	In a valley
Scalloway	7									
Chapel-le-Dale	25									
Dolgellau	28									
Blakeney	31									
Upper Beeding	47									

2.6 Urban Zones

This unit studies patterns within large settlements. It does this by dividing a typical British industrial town into **zones** – districts which have a particular function (e.g. housing) and may date from a certain building period (e.g. 1918–1939).

Like many northern towns, Chorley grew very rapidly during the Industrial Revolution. However, parts of its innermost zone – the **Central Business District** – date back to the fifteenth century. Shops and offices are just two of the many land uses at the town's heart. Around the C.B.D. is the **inner residential zone**. This was once an almost continuous belt of cotton mills, factories and terraced houses built during the nineteenth and early twentieth centuries. Now it is an interesting mixture of the old and the new. Its better quality terraces remain, but some pockets of demolished housing have been replaced with car parks, wider roads and small landscaped gardens.

Most British towns sprawled (grew outwards) very quickly between the 1914–18 and 1939–45 World Wars. Lower density semi-detached houses were popular at that time and their gardens and garages meant they used much more land than the old terraces. Post-war private and council-owned estates also have semi-detached houses, but bungalows are a common feature of these newer **outer suburbs**. Modern factories have tended to cluster together in special **industrial estates**. These are sited within easy reach of the main roads because lorries now carry over 90% of Britain's overland freight traffic.

Map Extract 8 : *Chorley*, 1:25 000 (1989)

Reproduced with the permission of the controller of H.M.S.O., Crown Copyright Reserved

Fig. 2.6A (1) *Chorley   The Central Business District around* GR583177

(3) *Chorley   A nineteenth century inner residential area around* GR590183

(2) *Chorley   An industrial estate around* GR595185

(4) *Chorley   An outer suburb around* GR571171

1 For each type of urban zone shown in Fig. 2.6A (1)–(4), describe its:
(a) general position within Chorley's built-up area
(b) street layout
(c) land uses (e.g. types and uses of its buildings; the nature of any 'open' spaces).

2 (a) Trace or draw very carefully the simplified land use map of Chorley shown below.
(b) Complete your map by shading its blank urban zones. The key and Map Extract 8 give you the necessary information.

Urban zone models

'Models' help us to understand the world we live in. Figs. 2.6C and D show two models based on land use patterns in urban areas. They cannot tell us exactly what any particular town should look like, but they do try to show the kinds of layout shared by many large settlements.

3 (a) Draw the two models shown in Figs. 2.6C and D as well as their shared key.
(b) Describe the zone pattern in each model.

(c) State how Chorley's zone pattern is both similar to and different from that in each model.
(d) On balance, which model layout seems to fit the Chorley pattern best?

Fig. 2.6C Mann's land use model

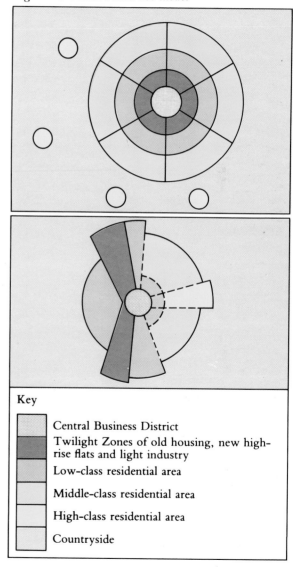

Fig. 2.6D Hoyt's land use model

Fig. 2.6B Chorley's urban zones

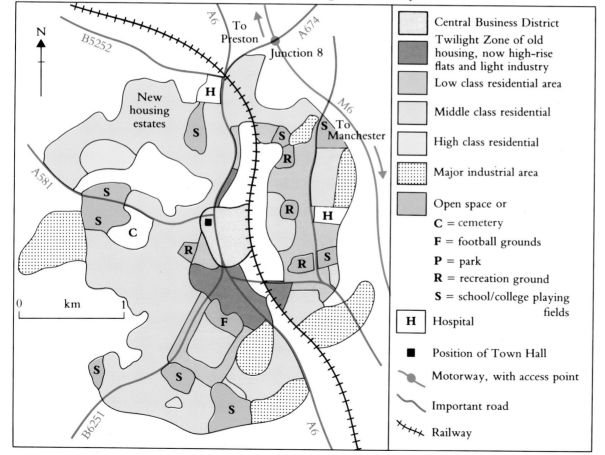

Key:
Central Business District
Twilight Zone of old housing, now high-rise flats and light industry
Low class residential area
Middle class residential
High class residential
Major industrial area
Open space or
C = cemetery
F = football grounds
P = park
R = recreation ground
S = school/college playing fields
H Hospital
■ Position of Town Hall
Motorway, with access point
Important road
Railway

Key
Central Business District
Twilight Zones of old housing, new high-rise flats and light industry
Low-class residential area
Middle-class residential area
High-class residential area
Countryside

3.1 Farming in the Fens

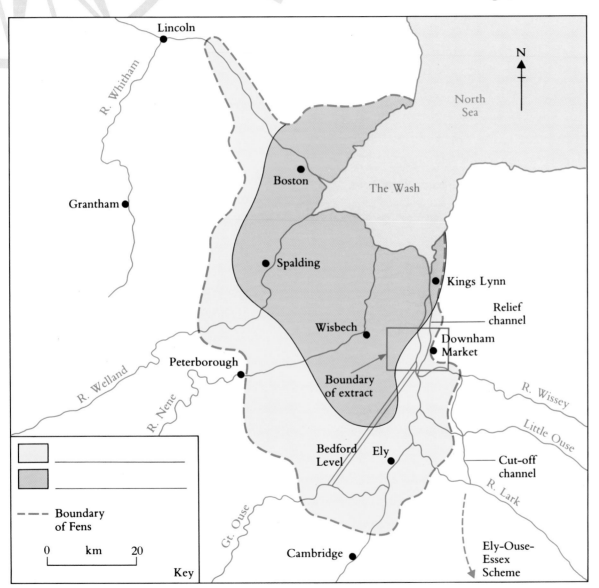

Fig. 3.1A The Fens

Key: North Sea, The Wash, Lincoln, Boston, Grantham, Spalding, Kings Lynn, Wisbech, Relief channel, Downham Market, Peterborough, Boundary of extract, R. Wissey, Bedford Level, Ely, Cut-off channel, R. Lark, Little Ouse, Gt. Ouse, Cambridge, Ely-Ouse-Essex Scheme, R. Welland, R. Nene, R. Whitham

Boundary of Fens

0   km   20

Key

Fenland is a low-lying part of Eastern England and used to have many reed-edged marshes. As its plants died and decayed, their remains built up a deep layer of fertile peat. Near the coast, the peat was later covered by silt transported and deposited by the sea.

The original Fenland was an unhealthy place to live in. Malaria-carrying mosquitos thrived in its stagnant water, and the local people became known as 'yellow-bellies' because of their discoloured skin! Such hazards did not stop people wanting to drain the area. They knew that the rich dark soil could produce very high **yields** (amounts of food), and even the Romans planned to drain parts of the Fens.

The seventeenth century saw the first major drainage scheme in the area. It was a partnership between the Duke of Bedford and a Dutchman called Vermuyden. The Duke owned large estates in the southern Fens and was able to finance the project. Vermuyden was an experienced engineer who had already drained similar areas in his own country. He knew that the Fens could only be farmed successfully by constantly removing the surplus water. The only large river able to do this naturally was the Great Ouse, but this followed a long, meandering course between Huntingdon and its estuary at King's Lynn (Fig. 3.1A). The agreed plan was delightfully simple.

It meant digging two parallel canals across the broad eastern loop of the Great Ouse. These would reduce its load of floodwater and provide extra ways for it to reach the open sea. Not surprisingly, their canals were named the New and Old Bedford Rivers! The northern ends of both 'rivers' are shown on Map Extract 9, close to the small village of Denver. The long strip of land between them was left as a **wash** – an area which could be swamped to save more valuable land elsewhere from flooding.

In 1953, freak weather conditions caused the Great Ouse to overflow its banks north of Denver. This led to the excavation of two more canals. The *New Cut* runs parallel to the Great Ouse between Denver and The Wash.

The other – called the *Cut-off Channel* – takes water from tributary streams before it can reach the Great Ouse. Denver is the key to this complicated network of waterways, and its **sluice gates** control the flow of water between them (Fig. 3.1B). Since 1971, some of the surplus water from this part of the Fens has been pumped southwards, helping to meet the water needs of people living to the north and east of London.

The Fenland scenery of today is one of flat land crossed by straight lines (Fig. 3.1C). Even some of the villages are linear in shape. The Fens are now very productive and its farmers specialise in growing wheat, barley and potàtoes. The farms are quite small by British standards – many are less than 25 hectares. Grazing land is confined to the

washes and the river banks.

The fields used to be drained by wind and then steam-driven pumps, but these have now been replaced by automatic electrically powered units. The constant draining of the Fenland peat has had a curious effect on the landscape. When dry, peat becomes crumbly and is easily eroded by the wind. Many farmers have planted lines of trees to act as wind-breaks, but these can only slow down the loss of the valuable topsoil. Much of the eroded material collects in the ditches which have to be dredged to stop them becoming blocked. Constant erosion means that some roads and buildings are now higher than the land around them – as Fig. 3.1D shows!

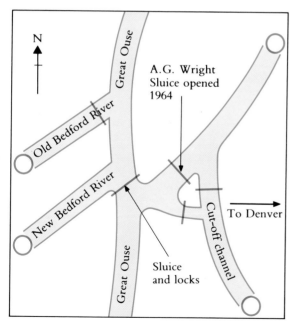

Fig. 3.1B The Denver Sluice complex

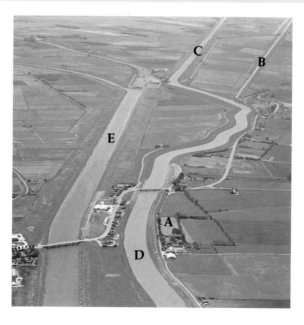

Fig. 3.1C Photograph for question 7

Fig. 3.1D Steps are now needed to get into this house!

1 Make a copy of Fig. 3.1A, then complete its key by writing 'Peat Fen' and 'Silt Fen' by the correct boxes.

2 (a) Describe the drainage work carried out by Vermuyden and the Duke of Bedford in the seventeenth century.
(b) Explain why it has been necessary to dig extra canals since then.

3 Write down each of these statements, then explain why each of them is true:
(a) Peat is the main soil in Fenland.
(b) Silt is found in the coastal areas.
(c) Fenland farms are usually smaller than the national average, and concentrate on growing crops.
(d) Animals are grazed in the washes and on the river banks.
(e) Most of the lowland field boundaries follow straight lines.
(f) The peat-covered fields are becoming steadily lower.
(g) Only one small area of the original marshy Fenland now remains. This is Wicken Fen, near the university town of Cambridge. (*Hint: consider land values, economic pressures and the location of Wicken Fen*).

4 Write down one local Fenland word meaning 'drainage canal' (see Map Extract 9).

5 What map evidence suggests that parts of the area in the extract have:
(a) been inhabited for several hundred years?
(b) created great wealth for the chief landowners?

6 (a) Write down the number of every spot height to the west of the River Great Ouse.
(b) Work out the average of all these spot heights.

(c) Repeat (a) and (b) for the area to the east of the river.
(d) Compare your two average heights.
(e) What effect does this height difference seem to have had on:
  –drainage patterns (of rivers etc)?
  –settlement patterns (i.e. where people choose to live)?
  –transport networks?
  –other types of land use (e.g. woodland)?

7 (a) In which general compass direction was the camera facing when the photograph in Fig. 3.1C was taken?
(b) Was this picture most likely to have been taken over square 5902 or square 6004?
(c) How can you tell where it was taken from?
(d) Name farm A on the photograph.
(e) Name waterways B, C, D and E – with the help of Fig. 3.1B.

8 Drivers wishing to travel from GR616033 to the north of Downham Market can use either the A10 or the B1507 roads. Suggest reasons why:
(a) there is a milestone by the side of the B1507, but not the A10.
(b) this stretch of the A10 was built to the east of Downham Market rather than its western side.

9 Like most small Fenland towns, Downham Market (population 5 000) is some distance from its nearest neighbour. This means it has to provide services for a large farming area as well as itself. List the various services it can offer, under these five headings:
(a) public buildings
(b) transport facilities
(c) water supply
(d) employment opportunities
(e) recreational facilities.

Fig. 3.1E Downham market

Map Extract 9 : *Downham Market, 1:25 000 (1985)*

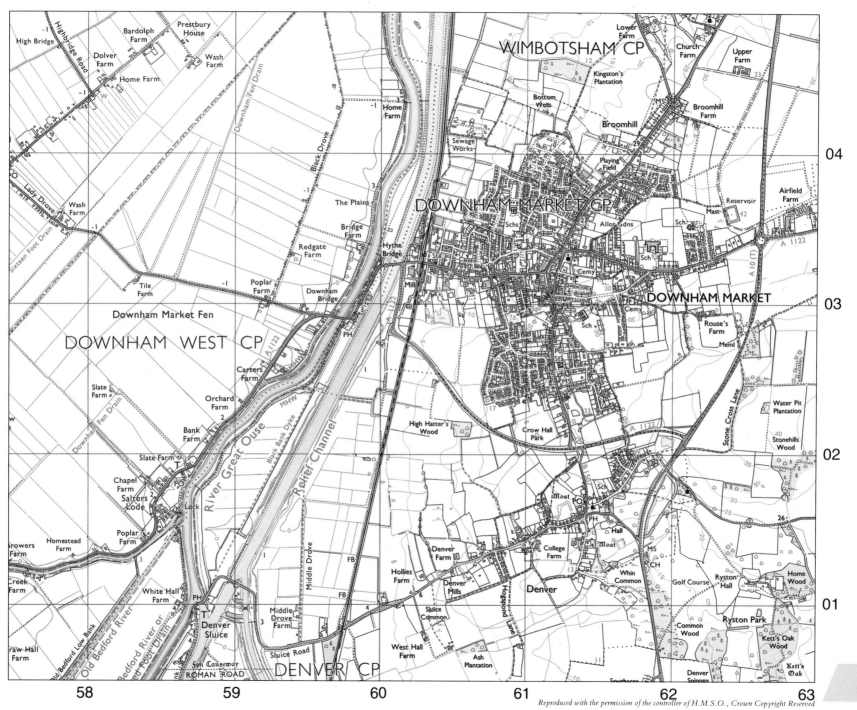

3.2 Valley Reservoirs

Britain's demand for fresh water has increased greatly in recent years. The need has been especially high in densely-populated, industrialised areas such as Teesside and Tyneside (Fig. 3.2B). In 1974, the government published its *Plan for Water*. This report recommended building valley reservoirs as the best way of meeting the increased demand. Kielder Water (Fig. 3.2A), which was completed in 1982, was a direct result of this report. Unfortunately the opening of Kielder Water coincided with the depression of the early 1980s and there is currently some over capacity in the area.

However, it may be necessary to flood more valleys in the North-East at some time in the future. This unit assesses the suitability of the River Tees area for valley-reservoir development. It then invites you to think about some of the issues raised by this method of storing water.

Fig. 3.2A Kielder Water

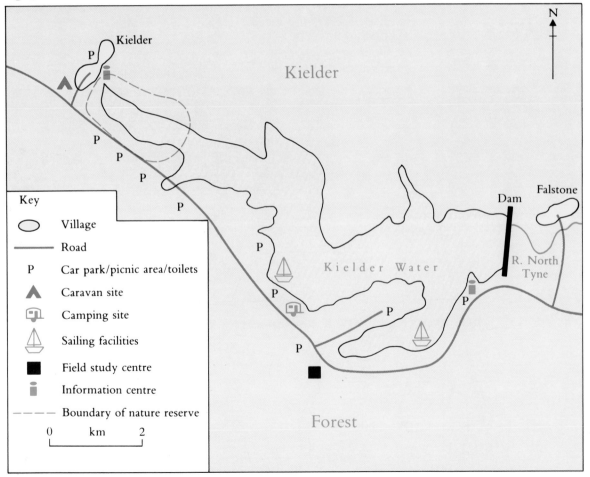

Key

- ⬭ Village
- — Road
- P Car park/picnic area/toilets
- ⛰ Caravan site
- ⊡ Camping site
- ⛵ Sailing facilities
- ■ Field study centre
- ᵢ Information centre
- --- Boundary of nature reserve

0　　km　　2

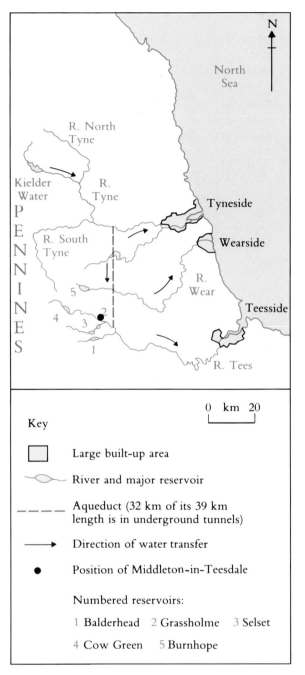

Key

- ⬜ Large built-up area
- ⬭ River and major reservoir
- --- Aqueduct (32 km of its 39 km length is in underground tunnels)
- → Direction of water transfer
- ● Position of Middleton-in-Teesdale

Numbered reservoirs:

1 Balderhead　2 Grassholme　3 Selset
4 Cow Green　5 Burnhope

0　　km　　20

Fig. 3.2B Major rivers and reservoirs in North East England

Ideally, a reservoir valley should:

- be in a region having a reliable supply of rainwater throughout the year. The area whose rain and tributory streams feed a particular river is called its **catchment area**.
- have impermeable rocks, as these do not allow water to escape underground.
- have hard rocks able to provide a firm foundation on which to build the dam.
- be narrow enough to build a short dam across it.
- be steep-sided. Narrow, deep reservoirs lose much less water through evaporation because of their smaller surface area.
- have a cool climate, since high temperatures also increase surface evaporation.
- have few inhabitants or business activities; both need to be compensated for the loss of buildings, land and trade due to flooding.
- have no railways or major roads near to the valley floor (where the flooding will be greatest).
- not have outstanding scenery or rare plant life.

1 What evidence in Map Extract 10 suggests that the River Tees area is suitable for valley-reservoir development? Consider the whole of the extract area, and discuss each of the nine key points listed above in turn.

Assume that the Northumbrian Water Authority wants to create a new reservoir in the upland area to the north of the River Tees; also that the Authority is unsure whether to flood part of Eggleston Burn valley, or use the Hudeshope Beck valley instead. It seeks your advice before taking this difficult decision. Questions 2–4 should help you to make a wise choice.

Size of Catchment Areas

2 Trace (or draw very accurately) a map of the Map Extract 10 area to show only:
   – the course of the River Tees
   – the courses of Eggleston Burn, Hudeshope Beck, and all the tributaries flowing into these two minor rivers.
   – the names of all three rivers
   – any streams belonging to the catchment areas of other rivers, even if these disappear off the edge of the map extract
   – two **watersheds** around the catchment areas of Eggleston Burn and Hudeshope Beck. These lines must enclose all the tributary streams of each river, and follow the highest land between it and the next catchment area. The spot heights and contour patterns will help you to do this quite accurately.

Valley Cross-sections

3 (a) Draw a relief cross-section along a direct line between GR932275 (at spot height 423m) and GR998273 (spot height 468m). The darker contour lines at 50m height intervals will give you most of the information needed to do this. Use a magnifying glass to pick out contour details in the valley bottoms.
(b) Label the two minor rivers with their names, then check that your cross-section is complete in every other way (see page 16).
(c) Compare the cross-sections of the two river valleys (i.e. width, depth and steepness of their sides). Look most carefully at the valley features below 350m.

Fig. 3.2C Rural Teesdale

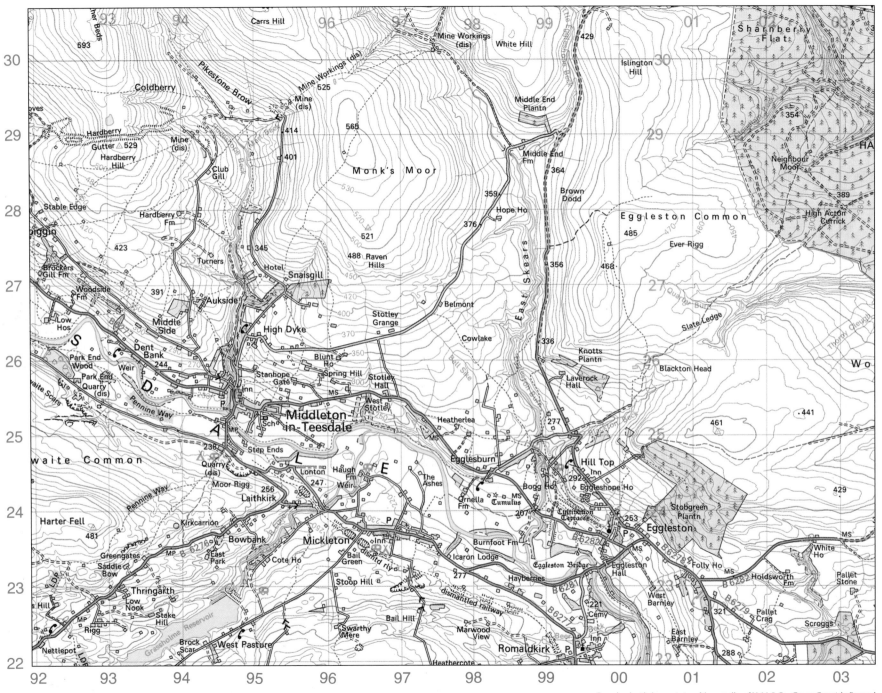

Land Uses

4 Describe the likely effects of flooding each valley along the GR932275–GR998273 cross-section to a height of exactly 350m above sea level. Take each valley in turn and write separate comments under these headings:
(a) housing
(b) business activities, including farming (see Fig. 3.2C).
(c) transport networks
(d) other land uses.

5 (a) After considering all the information you gathered for Questions 2–4, decide which of the two minor river valleys you would advise the Water Authority to flood.
(b) Summarize the three most important points which led to your decision in (a).

Inland reservoirs are official government policy, yet proposals to flood valleys often meet stiff local opposition; this is certainly true of areas which already have a number of reservoirs. Planning permission for a new dam cannot be given until at least one public meeting has been held. This is to give Water Authority experts and local residents a chance to exchange views.

In this case, Middleton-in-Teesdale would be the obvious place to hold any public meetings. It is quite a small village but does provide vital services for the rural area around it. The London Lead Mining Company created many jobs for the local people but closed down in 1905. Since then, Middleton's population has dwindled from 2 000 to only 1 200.

Fig. 3.2D Middleton-in-Teesdale

6 (a) Describe the distribution of the disused mine workings in the map extract.
(b) Explain why Middleton's location made it an ideal centre for the Teesdale lead mining industry.
(c) How might life in Middleton-in-Teesdale be affected if Eggleston Burn or Hudeschope Beck valleys are flooded?

Consider the village's economy as well as its people's opportunities for recreation. You must include both advantages and disadvantages in your answer.

Fig. 3.2E The disused Old Gang Lead Mine, north of Swaledale

3.3 A Dump on the Downs

The South Downs area of East Sussex is made up of two main types of rock. Each has its own kind of scenery, land uses and drainage (water movement) pattern.

Chalk scenery

Chalk is one of the easiest rocks to identify (Fig. 3.3A). It is bright white and fairly soft. Its tiny pores (spaces) allow water to seep slowly through the rock and be stored in it. There are few streams on chalk ridges, except where the **water table** reaches the surface (Fig. 3.3B). **Dry valleys** are however a common feature of chalk countryside. They do not usually contain a stream as the underground water is well below the surface. After very heavy rainfall, the water table may rise to the surface and allow streams to flow there again for a while. Such streams are known locally as **bournes** or **winterbournes**.

The soil on chalk cuestas (ridges) is thin and often covered by a short, coarse type of grass. These upland areas provide good grazing for sheep but many of the gentler slopes have now been ploughed up to grow cereal crops. Downland farms are large by British standards and need to use fertilisers to improve the quality of their topsoil.

Fig. 3.3A Exposed chalk on a Downland hillside

Clay scenery

Clay is even softer. When wet it becomes impermeable and can support a network of streams and rivers. It is easily eroded, so most clay areas are low-lying. Some are the bottoms of valleys which pass right through the Downs; others form **undulating** (gently rolling) plains – like the one in the northern part of the map extract. Although sticky, heavy and difficult to plough, clay does produce a crop of rich grass. It is therefore ideal for grazing cattle as well as sheep.

Fig. 3.3B Section across the South Downs

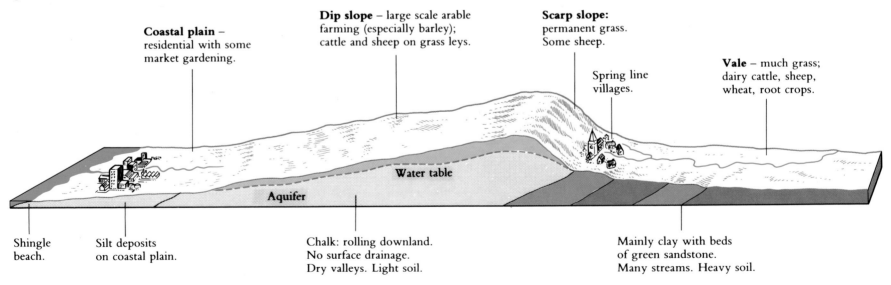

Coastal plain – residential with some market gardening.

Dip slope – large scale arable farming (especially barley); cattle and sheep on grass leys.

Scarp slope: permanent grass. Some sheep.

Spring line villages.

Vale – much grass; dairy cattle, sheep, wheat, root crops.

Water table

Aquifer

Shingle beach.

Silt deposits on coastal plain.

Chalk: rolling downland. No surface drainage. Dry valleys. Light soil.

Mainly clay with beds of green sandstone. Many streams. Heavy soil.

Fig. 3.3C Photograph for question 2

1 Pair up these key terms with their correct meanings: *Aquifer, Impermeable, Porous, Spring line, Water table.*

. . . describes a rock which allows water to seep through it.

. . . describes a rock which water cannot pass through.

. . . is at the height on a cuesta where streams begin to flow. This is because the water table reaches the surface there.

. . . is porous rock which is saturated with water.

. . . is the upper surface of an aquifer.

2 (a) Describe the landscape in Fig. 3.3C.
(b) Name the type of relief feature shown in the left hand side of this photograph.
(c) Explain how this type of feature was probably formed. You may need to discuss this in class first.

3 Copy out and complete this table:

The South Downs aquifer is used to supply water to the coastal towns of Sussex. The growth of these towns has greatly increased their demand for water. This in turn has affected the depth of the water tables in the area.

4 After class discussion:
(a) State how using aquifer reservoirs may affect their water table levels.
(b) Explain how changing water table levels affects the length of streams on the surface.
(c) Suggest possible advantages of using underground water supplies instead of surface reservoirs.

Britain's nuclear industry urgently needs a new disposal site for its low-level and intermediate radioactive waste. This would replace the present site at Drigg which is near to the waste reprocessing plant at Sellafield.

The South Downs area has some advantages for disposing of radioactive waste – even though parts of it are heavily built-up. Its rock layers are stable and so are not likely to disturb the waste after it has been buried. Chalk has very low levels of natural radiation and, in the lower areas; the clay would help to keep any contaminated water close to the chosen site.

A TABLE TO COMPARE CHALK AND CLAY AREAS		
Topic	**Description of chalk areas**	**Description of clay areas**
General relief	Has ridges called cuestas. These have a steep 'scarp' slope and a gentler 'dip' slope	
Rock features		
Population density and distribution		Most villages are on higher land where there is less chance of flooding. Large towns make the coastal strip more densely populated.
Land uses		

45

Factor	Data for low-level waste	Data for intermediate waste
Waste type and source	Mainly protective clothing, rubber gloves, etc worn by workers in nuclear power stations, hospitals and research laboratories	Mainly protective 'cladding' from around nuclear fuel rods. Other reactor components made of metal
Treatment	Waste material compressed into solid matter and packed in steel drums	Waste material broken down into small fragments then mixed with liquid concrete. When solid, stored in larger steel drums
Volume and transportation	250 cubic metres per week (= 45 lorry or 3 train loads, although sea transport can also be used)	48 cubic metres per week
Storage	All storage drums stacked 10m high in concrete-lined trenches. Full trenches sealed off with layers of concrete and then clay. This steel-concrete storage system should stop waste material escaping for at least 200 years. Site can be used as farmland again shortly after waste dumping completed	
Radioactivity	Radioactivity from intermediate waste can be 1 000 times more powerful than that of low-level waste. Intermediate waste may have a 'half-life' of up to 30 years (its radioactivity is halved every 30 years). The government's nuclear scientists assure us that the extra radiation from a new 'secure' site would be extremely small.	

Fig. 3.3D Disposal of low-level and intermediate nuclear waste

5 Assess how suitable the South Downs area is for disposing of low-level and intermediate nuclear waste. You should do this by discussing each of these important issues in turn:
–population density and distribution in this area
–local transport networks and facilities
–the different types of 'rock' in the area
–the locations of Britain's nuclear power stations
–the location of the waste reprocessing plant at Sellafield
–the national motorway and railway networks.

6 Imagine that three sites in the map extract area are being considered as nuclear waste dumps. They are at GR202075, GR258114 and GR271089.
(a) Note down the likely advantages and disadvantages of each site for this purpose.
(b) State briefly which site appears to be most suitable.
(c) Summarise the main reasons for your choice in (b).

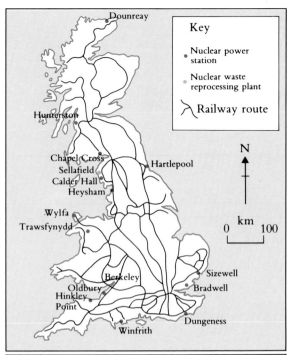

Fig. 3.3E Britain: nuclear power stations and the railway network

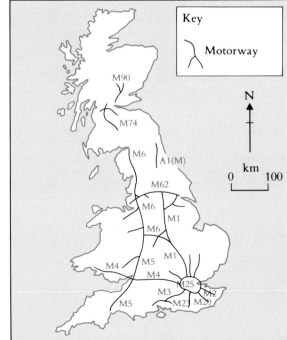

Fig. 3.3F Britain: the motorway network

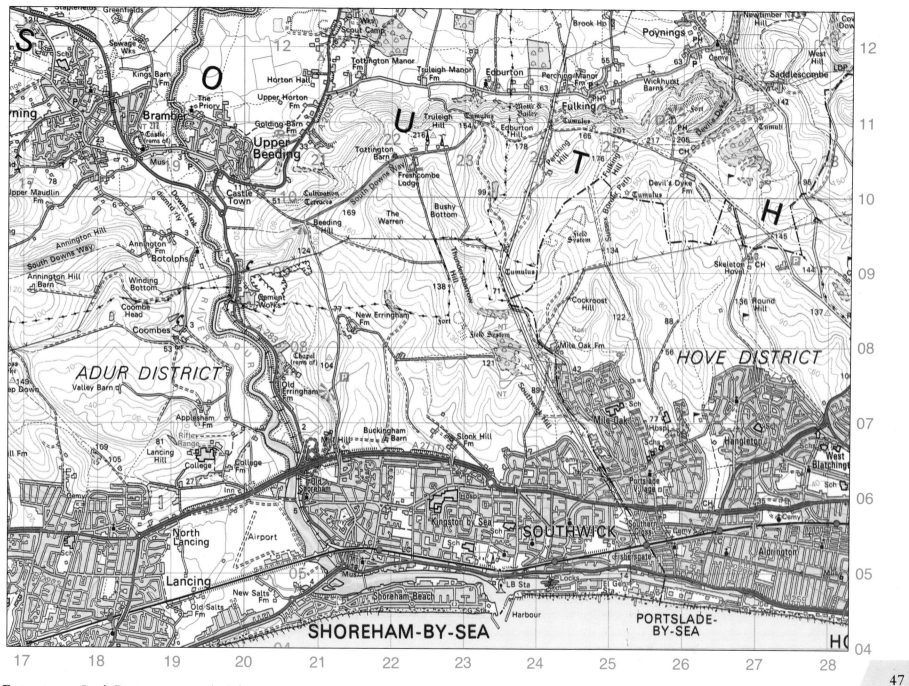

Map Extract 11 : *South Downs*, 1:50 000 (1987)

3.4 By-Passing a Village

People's attitudes towards transport developments have changed over the last 250 years. During the Industrial Revolution the rail and canal network developed and was a very important factor in the growth and prosperity of many towns. In twentieth century Britain, the growth of motor transport has made the railways far less important. It has also greatly affected the **quality of life** of people living near the busiest roads.

During the 1920s and 30s, the first **by-passes** were built to carry traffic away from built-up areas. In 1960, Britain's first stretch of motorway was routed around the east side of Preston (Fig. 3.4A). By-passes are still a popular way of reducing traffic congestion and the Department of Transport approves up to fifty new by-pass schemes each year.

1 (a) Plot this information as a line graph:

Year	UK car ownership – in millions
1955	3.0
1960	5.5
1965	9.0
1970	12.0
1975	14.0
1980	15.5
1985	16.8

(b) Describe the pattern shown by your completed graph.

2 Suggest reasons why:
(a) roads now carry far more passengers and cargo than the railways.
(b) by-pass roads are thought to be such a good idea. Here are some ideas to consider:
  –traffic flow
  –cost of land
  –present uses of land
  –pollution
  –annoyance.

3 Use the various maps in this book to show that each of these statements is correct. Give detailed information (e.g. town/ district/canal names and motorway M-numbers) whenever possible.
(a) Canals often lie well within built-up areas.

Fig. 3.4A Situation map of Broughton village

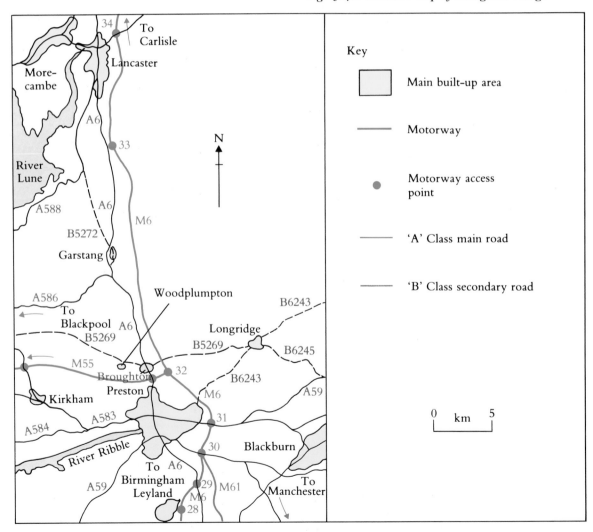

48

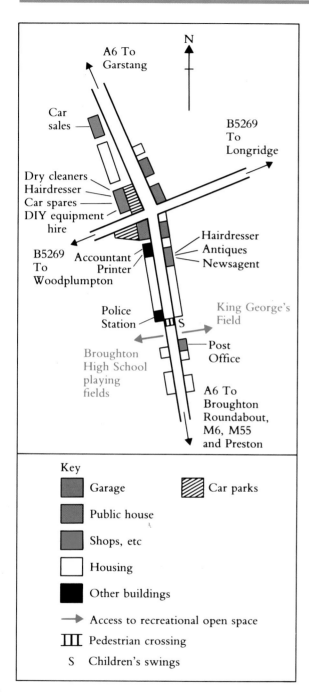

Car
sales

A6 To
Garstang

N

B5269
To
Longridge

Dry cleaners
Hairdresser
Car spares
DIY equipment
hire

Hairdresser
Antiques
Newsagent

B5269
To
Woodplumpton

Accountant
Printer

Police
Station

King George's
Field

S

Broughton
High School
playing
fields

Post
Office

A6 To
Broughton
Roundabout,
M6, M55
and Preston

Key

■ Garage   ▨ Car parks

■ Public house

■ Shops, etc

□ Housing

■ Other buildings

→ Access to recreational open space

Ⅲ Pedestrian crossing

S Children's swings

Fig. 3.4B Plan of Broughton village

It is likely that a by-pass will be built to the east of Broughton Village in the near future. There are a number of reasons why. 'Broughton Crossroads' is at the intersection of two busy roads – the A6 and the B5269 (see Fig. 3.4B). It lies to the north of Preston which is Lancashire's **county town** and therefore its main administrative centre. It is only 1 km from an even busier road junction, known locally as 'Broughton Roundabout', where the A6 is linked to both the M6 and the M55 motorways.

Junctions 32 and 33 on the M6 are 21 km apart. This forces southbound traffic from the Garstang area to pass through Broughton. The surrounding countryside is important for farming, but offers few other types of work; many of its people now **commute** (travel daily) to Preston, Blackburn and as far afield as Manchester. This has put increased pressure on Broughton Crossroads, and its traffic lights cannot cope during the peak early morning and late afternoon **rush hours**. A recent Annual Parish Report stated: "In the long term, the only possible solution to Broughton's traffic problems appears to be either a widening of the A6 or the building of a by-pass around the village".

Fig. 3.4C View of Broughton (taken before the rush hour to make the buildings easier to see)

49

(b) Railways are usually routed through – or very close to – town centres.

(c) Main railway stations were generally built on what was then the outer edge of the built-up area.

(d) Most motorways are routed around major built-up areas.

4 A recent traffic survey showed that over 80 per cent of vehicles using Broughton Crossroads do not turn off the A6 at that junction. What information from the text and Fig. 3.4A explains this very high percentage?

This study considers three alternatives:

Proposal A – a by-pass along route 'A' (see map extract)
Length: 2 km
Width: one lane in either direction
Northern access to the A6: new roundabout
Southern access to the A6: by-pass to lead directly onto Broughton roundabout.
Access to the B5269: nil, as a new bridge will carry the by-pass over the B5269 but not have slip roads to link the two.

Proposal B – a by-pass along route 'B'
Length: 1 km
Width: one lane in either direction
Access to A6 and B5269: by slip-roads, probably controlled by traffic lights.

Proposal C – widening the A6 through Broughton Village
Width: increase to two lanes in either direction. It has not yet been decided whether the extra space should be taken from the west, east, or both sides of the existing road.
Pedestrian crossing: replace the existing crossing at GR525349 by a subway, possibly at another point on the A6.
Effects on the B5269: some widening at the approaches to the crossroads, to provide more space for turning vehicles.

Name	Role	Location Number and Description
Miss Broadhead	Head Teacher	1 – Broughton High School
Mr Buller	Farmer	2 – Hoole's Farm
Mr Ford	Manager	3 – Kinder's Garage
Mr Black	Newsagents and	4 – Shop on A6
Miss Nugent	business rivals	5 – Shop on post-war housing estate
Mr Pane	Ambulance driver	6 – Broughton House (Headquarters, Lancashire Ambulance Service)
Mrs Proudfoot	Houseowner	7 – House on south side of B5269
Ms Shiner	Parent; walks children from home to school	8 – House
Mr Smiley	Publican	9 – Broughton Primary School
Mr Welcome	Club Steward	10 – Golden Ball Hotel
		11 – Broughton and District Social Club (which has tennis courts as well as indoor facilities)

5 Residents' reactions to the proposals
The table above provides basic information about ten Broughton residents whose names have been invented. Their role locations are however genuine, and are numbered both in the table and on the map extract.
(a) Which proposal(s) is/are most likely to appeal to each of the residents?
(b) Explain the choices made in (a) above by referring to each person's listed role.

Driver	Living . . .	Commuting . . .
Mr Ripper	in Woodplumpton	to Preston
Ms Smart	in Longridge	to Blackpool
Miss Speedy	by the A6, 3½ km north of Garstang	to Preston
Miss Swift	in Longridge	to Manchester
Mr Zest	in Preston	to Garstang (see map extract)

6 Commuters' reactions to the proposals
For each of the commuters listed in the table above:
(a) State which proposal(s) he or she is likely to find most attractive.

(b) Give at least one reason for each choice you have made in (a).

7 In the light of your answers to Questions 5 and 6:
(a) State which of the three proposals is best suited to the needs of both commuters and residents.
(b) Suggest whether Proposal C (if adopted) should be achieved by demolishing property:
 –only on the west side of the A6
 –only on the east side of the A6
 –on both sides of the A6
(c) Justify your answer to (b).
(d) Debate the statement: "Transport planners should always put the needs of commuters before the interests of residents". You could discuss the issue openly in class first.

Map Extract 12 : *Broughton*, 1:10 560. *This extract uses two maps dates 1968 (above grid line 35) and 1965 (below grid line 35)*

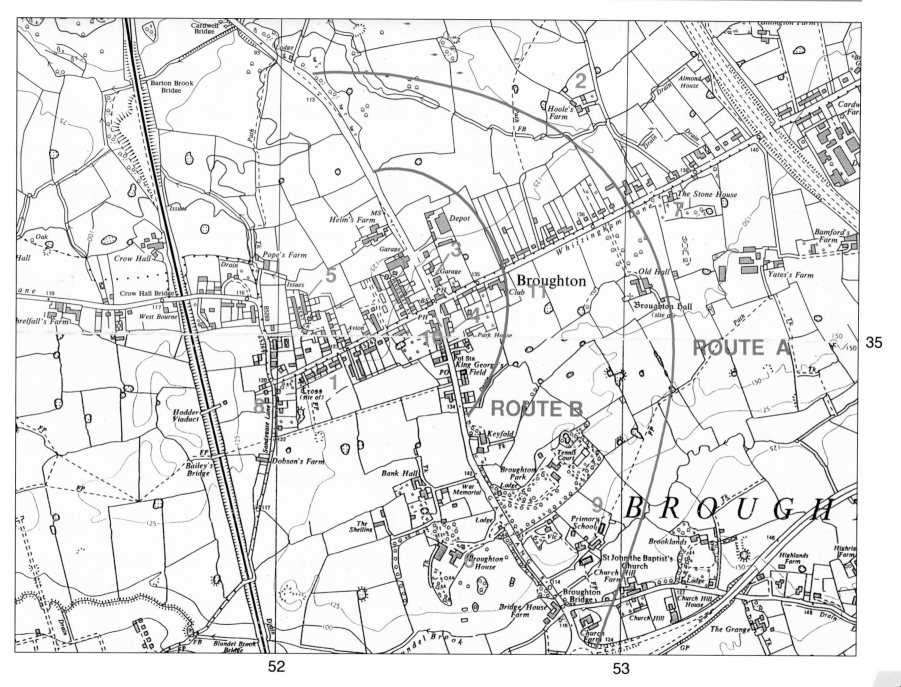

ROUTE A

ROUTE B

Broughton

BROUGH

3.5 Transport Networks

Accessibility describes how easy a place is to get to. Accessible places are very easy to reach, while inaccessible ones are not. This unit explains how to work out the accessibility of a place and the efficiency of a road network. The network in Fig. 3.5A is based on five imaginary towns. It is a **topological map** which means the **edges** (stretches of road between places) have been drawn as straight lines and not to scale. The most accessible town is where the most edges meet.

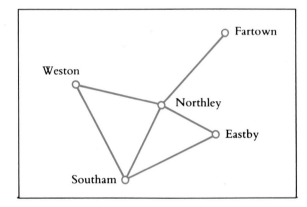

Fig. 3.5A Topological map for questions 1 and 2

1 (a) Make a copy of Fig. 3.5A, and shade all its edges in one colour and the towns (the **nodes**) in another. Add a simple key to state the meanings of the two colours you have used.
(b) Devise a table with two columns which shows the number of edges meeting at each node.
(c) Name the most and least accessible towns, according to your completed table.
(d) Near to which town in this network are business people most likely to want to build new factories?
(e) Give reasons for your answer to (d).

The **efficiency** of transport networks is also based on the number of edges within them. Completely efficient networks have a separate edge between every pair of nodes; the fewer the edges, the less efficient the network. This formula gives network efficiency as a percentage.

$$\frac{Number\ of\ edges\ in\ a\ particular\ network}{Number\ of\ edges\ in\ a\ completely\ efficient\ network\ with\ this\ number\ of\ towns} \times 100$$

2 (a) How many edges does the network in Fig. 3.5A actually have?
(b) What total number of edges must this network have to make it completely efficient?
(c) How many edges need to be added to make it completely efficient?
(d) What is the percentage efficiency of this network, as shown by Fig. 3.5A?
(e) What is the percentage efficiency of *any* completely efficient network?

3 (a) Re-draw Fig. 3.5B as a topological map.
(b) What is the percentage efficiency of this network?
(c) Name the most and least accessible towns in this network.
(d) Are the two towns you named in (c) the largest and smallest ones in the area?
(e) Comment on your answers to (c) and (d), adding possible explanations for them.

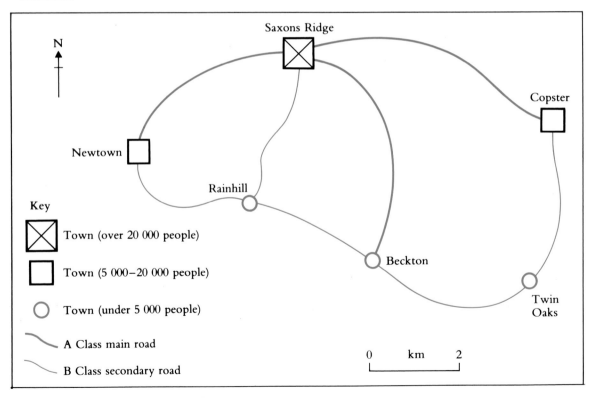

Fig. 3.5B Sketch map for question 3

3.6 Transport and Industry

1 Make a simple '*Diary of Events*' to show key events in Southampton's development as a port. You could use these two column headings:

Year, century or period	Description of event

2 (a) Identify Features A–G in Fig. 3.6A
(b) Describe the layout of Southampton Docks with the help of this photograph.

Fig. 3.6A Aerial view of Southampton

This unit studies port, industry and power station locations. It is based on Map Extracts 13 A and B and includes a major port, an oil refinery and a petro-chemical works.

The original site of Southampton (and now of its modern Central Business District) lies on a neck of land between the Rivers Test and Itchen; most of this area is just high enough to avoid serious flooding. The Normans quickly recognised the site's advantages, and had built a defensive wall around it by the year 1200AD. During the Middle Ages, a brisk trade in French wines and English cloth helped Southampton to grow into a sizeable port.

1836 was probably the most significant year in Southampton's long history, for it saw the opening of the port's first railway link with London. This meant that passengers and cargo arriving at Southampton could reach the capital much faster. The alternatives were to use very poor roads, or sail further east up the English Channel then back into the Thames Estuary. The Southampton Dock Company was formed in the same year and immediately began to improve the port's facilities. Its first main group of docks – known locally as the 'Old Docks' – were built on the shores around the town's ancient site. They were dug out of the rivers' soft clay and gravel banks. The 'New Docks' (completed in 1934 on reclaimed land) faced the River Test. Parts of its long, straight quayside stand out clearly in grid squares 4011 and 4111. Fifteen years later, an Ocean Terminal was opened on the western tip of dockland – in grid square 4208 – to cater for passenger and cruise liners like the *Queen Elizabeth 2*.

As well as handling thousands of passengers each year, Southampton imports timber and a wide range of foodstuffs (e.g. meat, fruit and flour). Her most important import is now crude oil. This is pumped ashore at Fawley, where super-tankers can berth at long, deep-water jetties. The oil is stored in huge tanks then processed at the refinery. Much of the refined oil is needed for the power station to the south-east and a petro-chemical works between it and Hythe; chemicals and synthetic (artificial) rubber are the chief products of this factory. A pipeline carries aviation fuel direct to London's Heathrow Airport. Other **port industries** include ship-building at Woolston, ship-repairing within the main dock area, and flour milling.

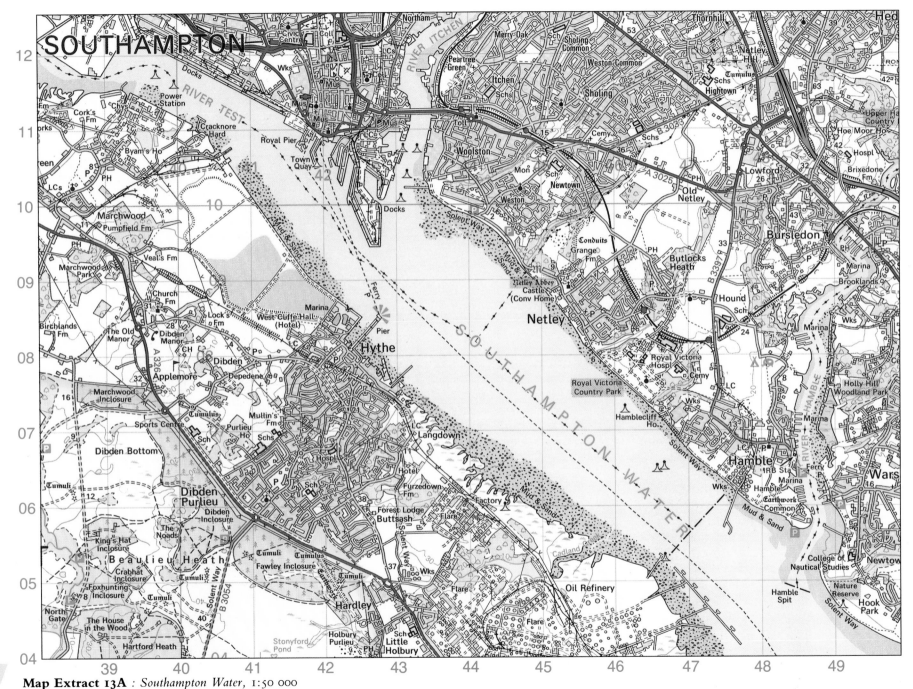

Map Extract 13A : *Southampton Water*, 1:50 000
(1986)

54

3 (a) Complete this table by putting ticks in the appropriate boxes. An atlas will help you to do this.

Port	Bristol	Hull	Liverpool	Plymouth	Southampton
Shortest direct distance from central London					
Well situated for ships trading with:					
Common Market countries*					
North America					
Scandinavia**					
Africa					

* especially France, Belgium and the Netherlands
** i.e. Norway, Sweden and Denmark

(b) According to your table, which of the five named ports has the best trading situation?
(c) What other factors, apart from general situation, could affect a port's growth and importance?

4 What O.S. map evidence suggests that:
(a) the River Hamble is a yachtsman's paradise?
(b) major industrial development is not likely to take place to the south and west of Dibden Purlieu (in grid square 4006)?
(c) many residents of Hythe work in Southampton?
(d) you could easily see the positions of Fawley Oil Refinery and the petro-chemical works to the north of it at night?
(e) house prices are certain to be much higher on the east shore of Southampton Water than the west?

(f) ocean-going oil tankers should not try to use the docks in grid square 4210 which lead into the River Itchen?
(g) it makes sense for Isle of Wight ferries to sail from Southampton instead of Calshot (which is much nearer)?
(h) Southampton's Central Business District is in the area around GR420120?
(i) the public house at Ashlett (in grid square 4603) is likely to have a lively trade, in spite of being in a small, isolated place?
(j) the needs of merchant ships – and their crews – are well catered for in the area shown in both map extracts?

5 (a) Make an enlarged copy of this skeleton graph

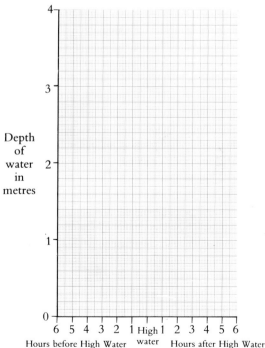

Depth of water in metres

Hours before High Water / High water / Hours after High Water

Map Extract 13B : *Fawley*, 1:50 000 (1986)

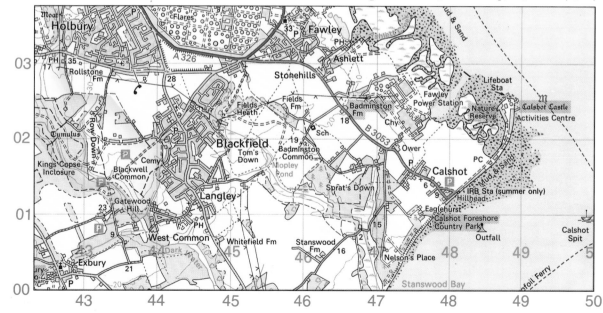

Location	Depth of water in metres												
	6	5	4	3	2	1	At high water	1	2	3	4	5	6
	Hours before High Water							Hours after High Water					
A typical British port	1.0	1.2	1.9	2.8	3.6	4.3	4.5	4.3	3.8	3.1	2.3	1.5	1.1
Southampton	1.9	1.7	2.1	2.6	3.5	4.4	4.5	4.3	4.4	4.2	3.3	2.7	1.0

(b) Plot this tabled information on it as two smooth, different-coloured lines.
(c) Add suitable labels to these lines, as well as a title for the completed graph. It could begin: 'A line graph to compare . . .'
(d) Describe the graph's tidal pattern for a typical British port.
(e) How is Southampton's tidal pattern different?
(f) Why has Southampton's unusual pattern helped it to become one of Britain's major ports?
(g) With the help of Fig. 3.6B, describe how the double-tides of Southampton Water are formed.

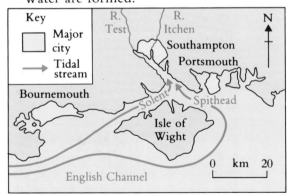

Fig. 3.6B Tidal movements around the Isle of Wight

6 All of these questions require you to think carefully, and write detailed answers. You may find it helpful to discuss them first in class.

(a) Suggest reasons why a large oil refinery was built at Fawley. You could consider factors such as general location, transportation, relief and cost of land.
(b) State whether the power station in grid square 3911 is most likely to be coal or oil-fired. Give reasons for your choice of fuel.
(c) The Central Electricity Generating Board (C.E.G.B.) plans to build a very large coal-fired power station immediately south-west of the oil-fired one in grid square 4702. The new station will occupy about 80 hectares, burn 5 million tonnes of coal and produce 1 million tonnes of ash every year. Both materials will be carried mainly by sea, via a specially built jetty, although road and rail transport will also be used from time to time. The station should employ about 3 000 workers during the construction phase, and 500 in the long term. How will building this power station affect the local area?

Fig. 3.6C Aerial view of the area to the south of Fawley

Fig. 3.6D Artist's impression of Fawley 'A' and the proposed Fawley 'B' power station

3.7 Urban Renewal

Urban renewal involves giving old built-up areas a fresh lease of life; for example, Fig. 3.7 A shows an area of Chorley that is scheduled for a renewal programme. **Urban degeneration** became a major problem for British cities after 1945, by which time a great many of their older Industrial Revolution buildings had become unfit for use.

Immediately after the Second World War, **comprehensive redevelopment** became the planners' favourite way of carrying out urban renewal. This meant demolishing whole districts then rebuilding them completely. The rows of terraced houses were often replaced by tall blocks of flats, until these became unpopular with residents during the 1960s and 70s.

Over the last twenty years or so, most town planners have opted for **renovation** rather than redevelopment. In renovated areas, only unsafe and very cramped houses are demolished. Public money is then used to improve the remaining housing stock by adding inside toilets and bathrooms, rewiring their electrical circuits and fitting new windows and doors. Some houses can be extended to provide extra living space. This new policy is less costly and helps keep local communities together. Renovation methods are not confined to housing; successful schemes have included redundant churches, cinemas and mills.

1 (a) State the meanings of the terms *urban renewal, comprehensive redevelopment, renovation* and *urban degeneration*.
(b) Say why urban renewal became more widespread after the mid-1920s.

2 After class discussion, give reasons why:
(a) high-rise blocks of flats are now unpopular with many of their residents.
(b) renovation is now more common than comprehensive redevelopment.

Fig. 3.7A Chorley town centre redevelopment area, viewed from the west

Fig. 3.7B Redevelopment site south of Chorley town centre

This study considers how a vacant piece of land in an area of urban renewal could be used in future. The land was originally occupied by an old cotton mill but this became a victim of the recession in the Lancashire textile industry and was demolished. The parcel of land lies 1 km to the north-east of Chorley town centre and its surroundings are shown in Map Extract 14. Six possible developments have been suggested for the site:

- a D.I.Y superstore similar to the one in Fig. 3.7B
- a housing development (mainly two-storey blocks of terraced houses)
- landscaped gardens, including a small play area suitable for young children
- a multi-storey car park with four levels
- an old peoples' home
- a day care centre

3 (a) Study the map extract carefully for about 10–15 minutes. Think of how nearby land uses might influence the site's development (e.g. old peoples' homes should be some distance from large factories).
(b) Debate your observations, taking each of the six suggested developments in turn. This can be done in small groups or as a whole class.

4 (a) List, in order of priority, the three suggested developments which you feel are most suitable for this site.
(b) Give a sound reason for each choice you have made.
(c) Now justify the order of priority you have given to the three selected proposals.

5 (a) Try to think of other uses to which this site could be put.
(b) Give at least two reasons to support each of these uses.

Map Extract 14 : *Chorley*, 1:10 000 (1985) *The redevelopment site is shaded pink.*

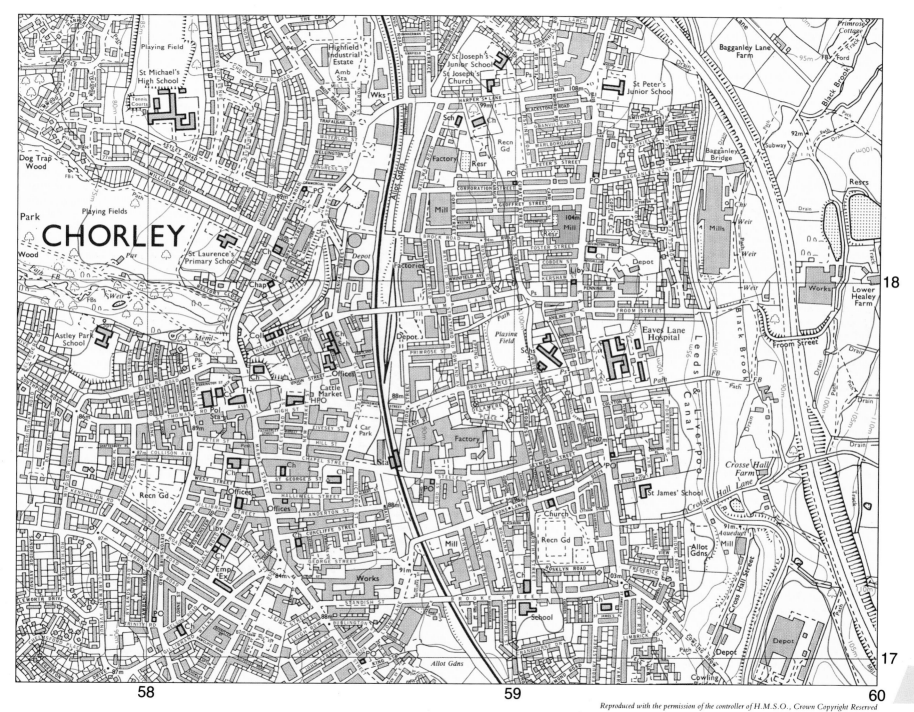

3.8 New Towns

Britain's towns and cities expanded very rapidly during the 1920s and 30s. Increased car ownership and people wanting to have a larger house with a garage and garden were important reasons for their growth. This worried some town planners a great deal. They knew that uncontrolled growth could link neighbouring settlements and create huge built-up areas. About the same time, many nineteenth century terraced houses near the town centres were coming to the end of their useful lives. These areas had to be renewed and some of their inhabitants – the **overspill population** – rehoused elsewhere.

New towns were the planners' answer to this problem. The New Towns Act of 1946 led to a series of these towns being built around London and other major British cities (Fig. 3.8A). Each new town was designed to take about 60 000 people and to be as self-contained as possible. That meant they would provide all the housing, services and jobs needed by the new arrivals. The individual housing estates were called **neighbourhood units**. Each one had its own primary school, church, parade of shops and 'village hall'. The planners thought this would help the people to settle in quickly, and not feel 'lost'.

Not all our new towns were intended to take city overspill populations, or located on **greenfield sites** in quiet, unspoiled countryside. A good example is Corby, described later in this unit. This particular new town was built onto an existing village and provided homes for workers at the nearby steelworks.

1 List the different reasons why new towns have been built in Britain since the Second World War.

2 Carefully explain the meanings of these key terms: *conurbation, greenfield site, neighbourhood unit, overspill population* and *urban sprawl.*

3 (a) Make a copy of Fig. 3.8A.
(b) With the help of an atlas, locate and name these important cities on your map: Belfast, Birmingham, Cardiff, Edinburgh, Glasgow, Liverpool, London, Manchester and Newcastle.
(c) Pair up each of these cities with at least one new town which is near enough to take its overspill population.

4 What are the likely advantages of building new towns onto existing settlements? Consider the viewpoints of both town planners and newcomers.

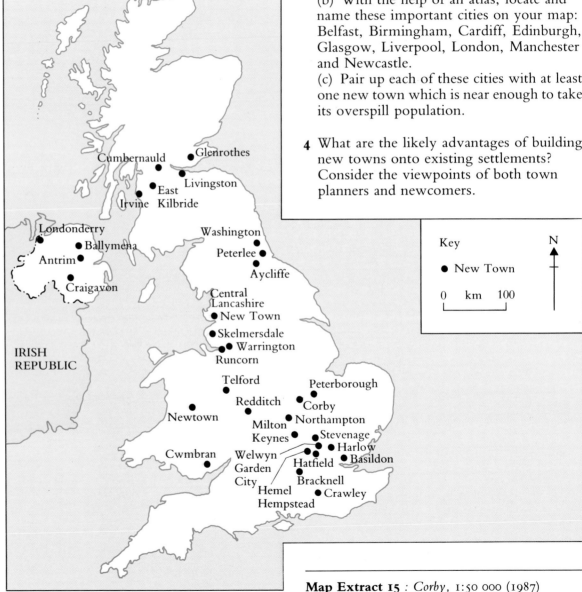

Fig. 3.8A New Towns in the United Kingdom

Key

N

● New Town

0   km   100

Map Extract 15 : *Corby,* 1:50 000 (1987)

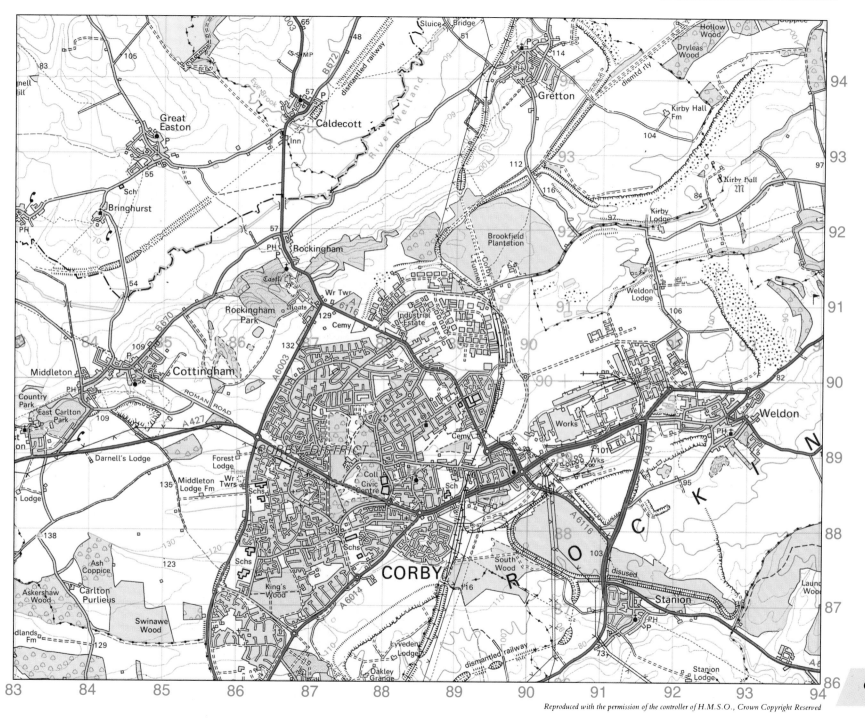

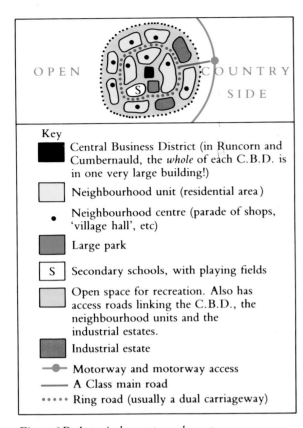

Key

■ Central Business District (in Runcorn and Cumbernauld, the *whole* of each C.B.D. is in one very large building!)

□ Neighbourhood unit (residential area)

• Neighbourhood centre (parade of shops, 'village hall', etc)

■ Large park

S Secondary schools, with playing fields

□ Open space for recreation. Also has access roads linking the C.B.D., the neighbourhood units and the industrial estates.

■ Industrial estate

●— Motorway and motorway access

— A Class main road

····· Ring road (usually a dual carriageway)

Fig. 3.8B A typical new town layout

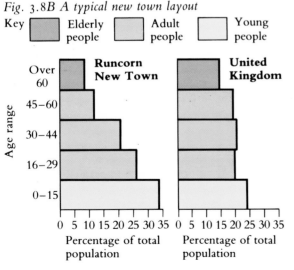

Fig. 3.8C Population pyramids

Corby used to be a small village of about 1 500 people. Its farmers lived in cottages clustered around the church, and one small blast furnace was its only industry of any size. This **smelted** iron from the Jurassic ores (see page 3) mined from beneath the rolling Northamptonshire countryside.

In 1933 a large *steel*-making plant was built at the edge of the village. This later expanded to become a fully **integrated** plant with its own coke ovens, blast furnaces, iron-steel converters, and steel rolling mills. The workforce increased very quickly and so did the demand for housing. Establishing a new town at Corby in 1950 was the government's way of helping it to cope with these changes. Unhappily, this period of expansion was very short-lived, for much of the steelworks closed down in 1980 with the loss of 5 500 jobs. Like other employment 'black spots' in Britain, Corby was given **Development Area** status to attract new industries. In Development Areas tax benefits, removal expenses and re-training allowances were offered by the Government to companies willing to build offices and factories there. A year later, these benefits were increased when parts of Corby were designated an **Enterprise Zone**. Such zones have fewer planning restrictions and do not pay local rates.

5 According to Fig. 3.8B, what are the main planning features of a typical British new town?

6 After class discussion, suggest what kinds of problems new towns might face:
(a) in the first few years, before the building programme is completed. Think about the town's facilities and its urban environment.
(b) in the long-term. Study Fig. 3.8C and consider both people and buildings.

7 State the most important reason for Corby's:
(a) original existence as a village
(b) early iron industry
(c) rapid increase in population in the mid-twentieth century
(d) growth as a new town
(e) status as a Development Area and Enterprise Zone.

Fig. 3.8D Corby New Town – Civic Centre

Fig. 3.8E Corby New Town – industrial estate

These questions are based *mainly* on Map Extract 15:

8 (a) How can you tell that many young families have already moved into Corby New Town?

(b) What is unusual about the stretch of the A427 main road between GR863892 and GR885882, compared with the other sections of main road in Corby?

(c) What is different about the position of the large school at GR893898, compared with Corby's other schools of a similar size?

(d) Why might Corby be described as a town which is 'inside out'? (*Hint: Look at grid squares* 8788 *and* 8789).

(e) Why might the inhabitants of Rockingham Village have been particularly worried by the building of a new town at Corby?

9 (a) Which part of Corby is most likely to have been the original village site?

(b) Give reasons for choosing this part.

10 Prepare a publicity handout for Corby Town Council which can be used to attract new industries and workers into the area. Its readers will want to know whether Corby:

(a) has good communications

(b) is convenient to other large towns (*Hint: use an atlas*).

(c) is surrounded by attractive countryside.

(d) is a modern but interesting town in which to live and raise a family.

11 (a) Draw a large sketch map of Corby's built-up area. Your layout should highlight these features: main roads, industrial areas, open space/recreational areas, residential areas, site of old village, the new 'town centre'.

(b) In what ways is your map of Corby both similar to and different from that of the typical new town in Fig. 3.8B?

Fig. 3.8F Corby New Town – new housing

Fig. 3.8G Corby New Town – original housing

Fig. 3.8H Aerial view of Corby New Town

Index